A String of Pearls

~ TREASURES FROM THE BIBLE ~

by

TIMOTHY J. E. CROSS
B. A., B.D., P.G.C.E., TH.D

AMBASSADOR

BELFAST ♦ **GREENVILLE**
NORTHERN IRELAND | SOUTH CAROLINA

ISBN   1 898787 95 6

AMBASSADOR PRODUCTIONS LTD,
Providence House
16 Hillview Avenue,
Belfast, BT5 6JR
Northern Ireland

Emerald House,
1 Chick Springs Road, Suite 206
Greenville,
South Carolina 29609
United States of America

DEDICATION

To Joe and Alice Wilson
with sincere thanks for welcoming me into their
hearts and home

CONTENTS

PREFACE

❖

In the following chapters we will explore some of the precious treasures of the Bible, treasures well known and treasures not so well known, but majoring all the time on *the unsearchable riches of Christ (Ephesians 3:8)*.

Although there are more versions and translations of the Bible around today than at any other time in history, sadly, the level of biblical illiteracy seems to be at an all time high, even amongst Christians. This book is my humble contribution to rectify the matter. Its preparation was a great blessing and my hope and prayer is that in reading it, you will find it to be the same.

Many of the following chapters first saw the light of day on the monthly *Quiet Corner* item which closes the South Wales Talking Magazine. I should very much like to thank those who have responded so favourably and kindly to these over the last years. Such encouragement often proved to be a real 'shot in the arm', and motivated me to share the fruits of my private Bible study with a wider audience by putting some of the messages into print.

Come then, and discover for yourself some of the precious and priceless pearls of the sacred Scriptures. The Lord Jesus Christ once told the following parables:-

The kingdom of heaven is like treasure hidden in a field, which a man found and covered up; then in his joy he goes and sells all that he has and buys that field.

Again, the kingdom of heaven is like a merchant in search of fine pearls, who, on finding one pearl of great value, went and sold all that he had and bought it. (Matthew 13:44-46).

Timothy J. E. Cross
Barry
South Wales

Chapter One

THE BOOK OF GOD AND
GOD OF ALL BOOKS

❖

Of making many books there is no end, and much study is a
weariness of the flesh (Ecclesiastes 12:12).

A ny student or author reading the above quotation will
heartily agree about the weariness of study. Most au
thors can remember the joy of having their labours in
print for the first time, but not before some considerable 'weariness of the flesh' during the long times of research and hours
spent at a desk writing or staring at the screen of a word proces-
sor. After the first draft comes the task of writing off to publish-
ers; there may be the disappointment of having the manuscript
rejected, but even the joy of acceptance will not bring exemption
from the long, careful and laborious task of proof-reading. The
thought of some authors writing and surviving over a hundred
books is quite awesome!

There is one Book however which towers above all other
books. Contrary to our quotation, instead of bringing weariness,

this Book brings rest, refreshment and nourishment to all those who will study it with a hunger for its words. This Book is the Book which will under-gird this book and the Book which should under-gird all Christian ministry. It is the Book of God and God of all books. I am referring of course to the Bible, the unique collection of the sixty-six specific books bound under one cover to make one Book. Here are some interesting facts about the Holy Bible: The Bible has:-1,189 chapters, 31,173 verses, 773,746 words and 3,565,480 letters.

The Bible is an incomparable Book because it alone claims to have been written by none less than Almighty God Himself, using human authors as His penmen and mouthpieces. It says of itself *All Scripture is inspired by God . . .* (2 Timothy 3:16) and that word 'inspired' literally means 'breathed out by God' – expired by the Spirit of God moving on the human authors.

You may have heard people say something like "If there is a God, then why doesn't He make Himself known?" Well the fact is that He has! The two lips by which God speaks are the Old Testament and the New Testament dividing the sixty six books which make up the Bible. The Bible is, if you will, God's love letter to all who will take it up humbly and read it believingly as such. Its whole message is summarised in perhaps its most famous verse, the 'Gospel in a nutshell' which reads *God so loved the world that He gave His only Son that whoever believes in Him should not perish but have eternal life* (John 3:16).

The Christian Faith is a Faith based firmly on the written Word of God. It is this written Word which leads us to the Living Word. This inspired Word leads us to the incarnate Word, the Lord Jesus Christ. One of the Bible's descriptions of Jesus is that of *'the Word of God made flesh'* (see John 1:14). Words are the outward expression and communication of our inward thoughts. This being so, how amazing it is to think that the eternal God has communicated to us His thoughts in the person of His Son, the Lord Jesus Christ. We just cannot truly know God apart from

Jesus Christ, and yet the Bible and Jesus are intertwined: All we can know of Jesus is what the Bible says about Him: when we read the Bible we see Jesus and when we see Jesus we see God.

Because the Bible has been written by God, it can do for us what no other book will ever be able to do for us. It says *the sacred writings are able to instruct you for salvation through faith in Jesus Christ* (2 Timothy 3:15). Peter similarly reminded his Christian readers *You have been born anew, not of perishable seed but of imperishable, through the living and abiding Word of God* (1 Peter 1:23). The Bible then is both a living and a life-giving Book. When its message is believed new life results! How imperative it is then to obey its injunction and *receive with meekness the implanted Word which is able to save your souls* (James 1:21).

The Psalmist wrote *For ever, O Lord, Thy Word is firmly fixed in the heavens* (Psalm 119:89) and the incredible durability of the Bible throughout the ages confirms this. No other book has such universal and international appeal. No other book is so suited to all the sorts and conditions of men and women. The Psalmist also wrote *The unfolding of Thy words gives light; it imparts understanding to the simple* (Psalm 119:130) and also *How sweet are Thy words to my taste, sweeter than honey to my mouth* (Psalm 119:103).

The Bible should be precious to every Christian. How precious is the Bible to you? The aim of *A String of Pearls* is to encourage you to seek the help of the God Who wrote the Bible to read, understand and enjoy the Bible that He has written. May your experience be Jeremiah's when he wrote of God's Word *Thy words were found, and I ate them, and Thy words became to me a joy and the delight of my heart* Jeremiah 15:16).

An anonymous Bible-loving Christian once wrote:-

This Book contains the mind of God, the state of man, the way of salvation, the reward of saints and the doom of sinners. Its histories are true, its doctrines holy, its precepts binding. It contains light to direct you, food to support you, comfort to cheer you. It is the traveller's map, the pilgrim's staff, the pilot's compass, the soldier's sword and the Christian's charter. It is a river of pleasure, a mine of wealth, a paradise of glory. Read it to be wise, believe it to be safe, practise it to be holy.

Oh wonderful, wonderful Word of the Lord!
Our only salvation is there
It carries conviction down deep in the heart
And shows us ourselves as we are
It tells of a Saviour, and points to the Cross
Where pardon we now may secure
For we know that when time and the world pass
away
God's Word shall for ever endure.

Chapter Two

THE GARDENS OF
THE BIBLE

❖

T he summer of 1992 saw the last of the series of National
Garden Festivals, held that particular year at Ebbw Vale
in South Wales. Visitors to Ebbw Vale - and they came in
their thousands - were all quite astonished at the plethora of the
most exquisite sights, sounds and smells. It was especially
astonishing considering that the colourful and perfumed site was
once the site of a large steelworks. The transformation of a
barren ground of toxic waste into a sight of such beauty could not
have been greater.

Gardens also figure in the Bible quite prominently, and a
'guided tour' of them is both interesting and instructive. According to the Bible, human history began in a garden. In the opening
chapters of the Bible we read how the *Lord God planted a garden
in Eden, in the East; and there He put the man whom He had*

formed. And out of the ground the Lord God made to grow every tree that is pleasant to the sight and good for food . . . (Genesis 2:8,9). What a garden that was. There, Adam and Eve lived in the perfect environment and enjoyed perfect harmony and fellowship with their Maker. Was, however, is the apposite word, as if you know the scenario, you know that this harmony and perfection was not to last. Sin entered into the garden and Adam and Eve lost their fellowship with God their Maker. God cursed the ground, and thorns and thistles appeared as well as the nicer plants. Finally, in an act of just punishment, God banished Adam and Eve from the garden.

History however, not only began in a garden, but also, in two gardens, history took on a drastic turn. Not long before His death on the cross Jesus entered into a garden – the Garden of Gethsemane on the Mount of Olives in Jerusalem. In Gethsemane Jesus contemplated the awful suffering He was about to undergo to save God's people and restore them to the original harmony with Himself. The horror of it all was indescribable. The sinless One was about to bear the sins of all of God's people upon His own sinless self. Can you imagine that? (I shudder at the thought of His bearing just my sins, let alone the sins of all God's elect.) No wonder that in that garden Jesus fell down to the ground and prayed most earnestly *Father, all things are possible to Thee; remove this cup from Me; yet not what I will but what Thou wilt* (Mark 14:36). The will of God was indeed that Jesus should suffer. Jesus was obedient to God's will, and so He went to the cross and shed His precious blood, so that whoever believes in Him may receive the forgiveness of sins and peace with God forevermore. Jesus died that we might live, and this leads us into another garden central to Scripture:-

John 19:41 ff. reads:- *In the place where He was crucified there was a garden, and in the garden a new tomb where no one had ever been laid. . . as the tomb was close at hand they laid Jesus there.* This garden is the most important and epochal garden in the history of the world. It was in this garden that Jesus broke the bonds of death and hell. This garden - the garden owned by Joseph of Arimathea - was the garden of the resurrection. Scripture proclaims *He was raised on the third day in accordance with the Scriptures* (1 Corinthians 15:4), bringing new life and new hope to all who believe.

History, then, began in a garden. History took a dramatic turn in a garden. Turning to the last chapter of the Bible though, we see that history will end in a garden for all who believe in Jesus. Revelation 22 gives us a glimpse into the eternal glory and blessedness of the redeemed – and it describes it as being like a beautiful garden city:- *Then He showed me the river of the water of life, bright as crystal, flowing from the throne of God and of the Lamb . . . also on either side of the river, the tree of life with its twelve kinds of fruit, yielding its fruit each month; and the leaves of the tree were for the healing of the nations. There shall no more be anything accursed . . .* (Revelation 22:1 ff.).

How wonderful. How delightful. If we belong to Jesus, no matter what our lot in this life may be, one day we will live in a beautiful garden – Paradise. In Paradise all the thorns and thistles of this world will be gone, and we will know and enjoy perfect peace and live in perfect harmony with God and one another for all eternity. The big question is then, Are you heading for this garden? The only entrance to it is by way of the other two gardens mentioned, Gethsemane and the Garden Tomb, for it is only by personal faith in the Saviour Who died and rose again that we can be sure that our sins are forgiven. This alone is the pardon that leads to Paradise.

May the *Lord guide you continually and satisfy your desire with good things, and make your bones strong; and you shall be like a watered garden, like a spring of water, whose waters fail not* (Isaiah 58:11).

Chapter Three

THE BLOODSTREAM OF
THE BIBLE

❖

"It may be just a smear to you, but it's a matter of life and death to someone else!" said Tony Hancock in his manic, nervous tone to 'Dr McTaggart', when he went to give blood in the classic comedy *The Blood Donor.* Seriously though, blood is, of course, a matter of life and death:-

> Blood is a very active tissue. It carries nutrients, oxygen, hormones, waste products and antibodies from one organ to another. It connects the different parts of the body and is therefore described as a connective tissue. . . The average individual has about five to six litres of blood circulating. . . (P. 68, *Anatomy and Physiology Applied to Nursing,* Janet T. E. Riddle, Churchill Livingstone, 1985).

Did you know that the Bible is a blood-stained book? It mentions blood some 457 times to be precise, and the New Testament deliberately uses the term 'the blood of Christ' three times more often than the term 'the cross of Christ' and five times more often than the term 'the death of Christ'.

An event central to the Old Testament is the 'Exodus' from Egypt. In this the people of Israel escaped from the angel of death by the application of the *blood* of the Passover Lamb to the doors of their houses. God said to them reassuringly *when I see the blood I will pass over you* (Exodus 12:13). Then if we skip many centuries and turn to the last book of the Bible, we do not get far beyond the opening verses of Revelation when we read the praise *To Him Who loves us and has freed us from our sins by His blood* (Revelation 1:5).

Blood, as we have already mentioned, is absolutely vital to life. It is essential in that it takes food and oxygen to the cells of our body. Blood in the Bible however speaks not so much of life but of life given – life given up in death. Every Jew would have known this, as every time an innocent animal was sacrificed and its blood shed, God's words to them would have been recalled: *the life of the flesh is in the blood, and I have given it for you upon the altar to make atonement for your souls; for it is the blood that makes atonement by reason of the life* (Leviticus 17:11).

Yes, blood is essential for life, but blood – or more specifically, faith in the blood of Jesus – is essential for eternal life. Without it we will be spiritually dead. The blood of Jesus is God's way of salvation. Life comes to us through the blood of Christ. Blood meant death for Him, but it means life for all who believe in Him. Jesus explained His impending death as follows: *This is my blood of the new covenant which is poured out for many for the forgiveness of sins* (Matthew 26:28), and a lovely old hymn brings out the contrast between the many sacrifices of the Old Testament and the one sacrifice of Christ Himself so:-

Not all the blood of beasts
on Jewish altars slain
could give the guilty conscience peace
or wash away the stain

But Christ the heavenly Lamb
takes all our sins away
a sacrifice of nobler name
and richer blood than they.

The Bible teaches that we have *propitiation by His blood* (Romans 3:25) – propitiation means 'to turn aside God's wrath'. God is angry with sin, but the blood of Jesus - His sacrificial death in our place - appeases, satisfies and stays the wrath of God due to us.

The Bible teaches that we are now *justified by His blood* (Romans 5:9), which means that the blood of Jesus frees us from sin's condemnation and declares us righteous in God's sight.

The Bible says that we are *brought near in the blood of Christ* (Ephesians 2:14) for it is through the blood of Jesus that guilty sinners are enabled to approach a holy God with confidence, knowing that He will not condemn us for our sins. God is at war with sinners, yet the Bible assures us that Jesus made *peace by the blood of His cross* (Colossians 1:20).

The theme of the blood is inexhaustible, but lastly, did you know that the Bible teaches that we have cleansing by the blood? At first this seems very strange, as we all know that blood tends to stain rather than cleanse. Yet if we know our biology, we will know that blood takes away harmful waste products from our cells, as well as taking food and oxygen to them. In the spiritual realm, there is no more harmful product than sin, as it is sin which separates us from God and, if unforgiven, will cast us into hell. How heartening then is the Bible when it declares that *the blood of Jesus His Son cleanses us from all sin* (1 John 1:7).

Blood certainly is not for the squeamish and is certainly not a topic of normal daily conversation. Such reservations about blood will soon vanish if we are in need of a life-saving blood transfusion though. Similarly, without the Holy Spirit's awakening of us to our peril, we will never be interested in the blood of Jesus. Yet once we are awakened to our spiritual need, we are awakened to our need of the blood of Jesus. We will realise that we are all sinners and that it is only the blood of Jesus that can assure us that our sins are forgiven and that we have peace with God both here and hereafter.

> The blood has always precious been
> 'tis precious now to me
> Through it alone my soul has rest
> From fear and doubt set free
>
> Oh wondrous is the crimson tide
> which from my Saviour flowed!
> And still in heaven my song shall be
> "The precious, precious blood".
>
> Not all my well remembered sins
> can startle or dismay
> That precious blood atones for all
> and bears my guilt away.

Chapter Four

THE TREES OF
THE BIBLE

❖
————————————————   ————————————————

I t is only when you move to a road without any trees that you
begin to like and miss them. They give a road character and
provide welcome shade on hot days. Certain trees can prove
too much of a temptation to either children or cats – as any
casualty department or fire service will confirm. Those of us who
grew up with apple trees in our back garden come to think that,
like people, they are very unpredictable – some years their
branches are weighed down with fruit, whilst in other years, for
no apparent reason, they bear no fruit at all.

Trees also figure quite prominently within the pages of the
Bible. Jesus once said that the kingdom of God is like a grain of
mustard seed which a man took and sowed in his garden; and it
*grew and became a <u>tree,</u> and the birds of the air made nests in
its branches* (Luke 13:19) – which suggests that although the

kingdom of God had seemingly insignificant and small begin-
nings, one day it will expand to have world dominion, and people
from all nations will find rest in it. Let us consider three Bible
trees which 'grew' at important epochs in Biblical history:-

The Tree of Pain

Sadly, the 'root' of all pain and sorrow in the present world
can be traced back to a tree. Sin and its consequent misery originated with our first ancestor, Adam, who, at the dawn of world
history, committed the first ever offence against God in the garden of Eden. The book of Genesis relates how both Adam and
Eve had the audacity to sin against God and eat from the forbid-
den fruit of the tree of the knowledge of good and evil. God had
stated quite plainly *You may freely eat of every tree of the garden;
but of the tree of the knowledge of good and evil you shall not eat,
for in the day that you eat of it you shall die* (Genesis 2:16).
Adam's subsequent rebellious eating from this tree brought spiritual death on both himself and us (see Romans 5:12), ruining
both his and our relationship with God our maker. Adam's action
rendered Eden's tree a tree of pain.

The Tree of Pardon

On a happier note, the 'root' of redemption can also be
traced back to a tree – the tree of Calvary, where Christ, the Last
Adam, died to procure the sinner's pardon. Redemption was
wrought on the cross of Calvary by the Christ of Calvary. This
cross however was very different from the ornate jewellery worn
around some people's necks and very different even from the
carved emblems seen in some churches. The original cross was a
cruel, rugged plank of wood, cut with no frills from a weather
beaten tree.

They put Him to death by hanging Him on a tree (Acts
10:39) preached Peter to the Gentiles. Years later, Peter explained

the meaning of Christ's crucifixion somewhat further by stating that *He Himself bore our sins in His body on the tree* (1 Peter 2:24). The apostle Paul likewise was adamant that *Christ redeemed us from the curse of the law having become a curse for us, for it is written 'cursed be everyone who hangs on a tree'* (Galatians 3:13). In Biblical times, hanging someone on a tree was indeed evidence of their being under God's curse. The Law had stated such: *if a man has committed a crime punishable by death and he is put to death, and you hang him on a tree, his body shall not remain all night upon the tree, but you shall bury him the same day, for a hanged man is accursed by God* (Deuteronomy 21:22,23).

Christ then was cursed so we might be blessed, and have God's curse upon us for our sins removed. The tree of pain in the garden and the tree of pardon at Golgotha. What a contrast there is between the two. Augustine once said:

> As we have been made dead by a tree, so we have been made alive by a Tree; a tree discovered to us our nakedness, and a Tree covered us with leaves of mercy.

We can never exhaust the contents of the Tree of Calvary. The Tree of Calvary had one base on the earth whilst its top pointed up to heaven and the cross does indeed connect earth and heaven when we put our faith in the One Who died upon it. Jesus is the *one mediator between God and men* (1 Timothy 2:5). The hymn writer was right when he wrote 'so seems my Saviour's cross to me, a ladder up to heaven'.

The Tree of Calvary extended four ways – north, south, east and west. Christ's redemption too extends to His elect from all corners of the earth. Jesus explained how *men will come from east and west, and from north and south , and sit at table in the kingdom of God* (Luke 13:29). Revelation too relates this *great multitude which no man could number, from every nation, from all tribes and peoples and tongues* . . . (Revelation 7:9).

On the tree of Calvary Christ's arms were stretched out wide, as cruel men nailed Him mercilessly to the wood. Christ's outstretched arms speak of His welcome. Jesus welcomes sinners! *This Man receives sinners and eats with them* (Luke 15:2). Do you know that you are a sinner? Do you know that Jesus receives sinners? Do you know that Jesus saves sinners? Do you know that Jesus embraces sinners – just like the father of the prodigal who in seeing his rebellious but repentant son *had compassion and ran and embraced him* (Luke 15:20).

The Tree of Paradise

The trees of Eden and Calvary are two of the most significant trees of Scripture. The tree of Eden is the tree that leads to hell, but the tree of Calvary is the tree that leads to heaven for all who believe in Jesus. Interestingly, the Bible reveals that there will even be trees in heaven. In the very last chapter of the Bible, when he relates the very epitome and fullness of eternal life, John describes: *on either side of the river the <u>tree</u> of life with its twelve kinds of fruit, yielding its fruit each month; and the leaves of the tree were for the healing of the nations. There shall no more be anything accursed* . . . (Revelation 22:2,3). We can only have this blessed tree of glory in heaven if we 'have' the bloodstained tree of Golgotha on earth.

> O tree of glory, tree most fair
> ordained those holy limbs to bear
> how bright in purple robe it stood
> the purple of a Saviour's blood
>
> Upon its arms, like balance true
> He weighed the price for sinner's due
> the price which none but He could pay
> and spoiled the spoiler of his prey.

Chapter Five

THE EDUCATION OF
THE BIBLE

❖

Education never seems to be far from the news headlines. It causes a lot of hot air because so many people and their children are affected by it. It can even sway the way people vote politically. Published surveys revealing just how few seven year olds can read, along with complaints from employers about the unsuitablity of school leavers and even university graduates for their posts, causes raised eyebrows and 'tut tutting.' School teachers at times seem to come in for as much animosity as traffic wardens and tax men!

The philosophy of education seems to have changed a great deal since the more regimented junior school days of a generation or so ago. Classrooms full of children do not seem to have the enforced silence of earlier years; tables arranged in groups seem to have replaced the rows of desks which all faced the front, and the good old 'stock room' seems to have been replaced by the 'media resources unit.' The different philosophies apart though, the main emphasis is still on the so called 'Three R's' – reading, writing and arithmetic – as apart from the three R's any further progress in education is well nigh impossible. The three R's are literally 'primary' and essential for a good educational foundation.

I should like to draw your attention to the three R's of the Christian Faith, as taught in the Bible, the basic textbook of the Christian Faith. Again, just as in the world of education, apart from these three R's Christianity is not Christianity, and without them we will not even begin our Christian journey, let alone arrive safely in heaven. These three R's are:- 1. Our Ruination by Sin 2. Our Redemption by the Saviour and 3. Our Regeneration by the Spirit.

1. Our Ruin

From the Bible's standpoint, the bad news always precedes the good. Christianity centres on the Person of Christ, but the bad news is that we desperately need Christ because we are ruined; that is, our relationship with God is ruined because of our sin – who we are and what we do. In schools, you do not have to teach children to be naughty. Lessons in misbehaviour are unnecessary as it comes naturally to them. Similarly, we do not have to be taught how to displease God by breaking His commandments. It comes naturally to us. King David admitted *Behold I was brought forth in iniquity and in sin did my mother conceive me* (Psalm 51:5). When Adam sinned in the Garden of Eden he ruined the beautiful harmony he had with his Maker – and the terrible thing is that we, his descendants, are just like him. The Bible states that *as sin came into the world through one man and death through sin, and so death spread to all men because all men sinned . . .* (Romans 5:12). Without Christ we are ruined.

2. Our Redemption

The name 'Jesus' means saviour or rescuer. *Christ Jesus came into the world to save sinners* (1 Timothy 1:15). In Jesus, our ruined relationship with God, caused by sin, can be salvaged and restored. Go to most Christian churches and you should hear the preacher preaching about the cross. The cross is the heart of the heart of Christianity, as it was on the cross that Jesus shed His precious blood so that the sin which separates us from God can be forgiven, and we can be restored to harmony and fellowship with Him. 'Redemption by the blood of Jesus' almost encapsulates the whole of the Christian Faith. *In Him we have redemption through His blood, the forgiveness of our trespasses according to the riches of His grace* (Ephesians 1:7). That we can be redeemed from our ruin is the Christian Good News:-

Redeemed how I love to proclaim it
Redeemed by the blood of the Lamb
Redeemed through His infinite mercy
His child and forever I am.

Our Christian education is not quite complete however. We need not only to consider our ruin and redemption, but also:-

3. Our Regeneration

Regeneration refers to being made alive – being brought to life spiritually by the Holy Spirit of God. You may ask why everyone is not alive to the fact of their ruin by sin and the promise of redemption by the Saviour? The unpalatable answer is because salvation is God's work and not ours – He chooses to save some whilst He passes over others. Salvation only becomes a reality in a person's life when God the Holy Spirit works inwardly on their soul, awakening them to their lost, ruined condition and revealing the complete remedy for sin in Jesus. The Holy Spirit even gives us the necessary saving faith in Jesus which makes the redemption He wrought our own. We are as completely dependent on God's Spirit to apply salvation to us as we are on God's Son to accomplish salvation for us. Regeneration is God's work. He alone gives spiritual life just as He alone can give physical life. (You will not remember giving God your permission for you to be born!) *It is the Spirit that gives life, the flesh is of no avail* (John 6:63). The Holy Spirit alone can *convince the world concerning sin, righteousness and judgement* (John 16:8). Apart from the Holy Spirit, we would never be able to trust in Jesus and receive the eternal life He gives.

The three R's of the Christian Faith. Our Ruination by sin, Redemption by the blood of Jesus and our Regeneration by the Holy Spirit.

In school, only the cleverest reach the top, as the whole system is based on merit. How good then that God's salvation is based on His mercy and not our merit. God reveals Himself to all who humbly trust in Him, whether they be clever, mediocre or dim. God reveals Himself to those who come dependently to Him as a child comes to a father. Jesus said:- *I thank Thee Father, Lord of heaven and earth, that Thou hast hidden these things from the wise and understanding and revealed them to babes. Yea Father, for such was Thy gracious will* (Matthew 11:25,26).

Chapter Six

THE RIVERS OF
THE BIBLE

❖

Most of the towns and cities in Britain can boast of having at least one major river. Cardiff actually has three – with some beautiful walks to be had along the banks of the River Taff. At Aberystwyth you could watch the River Ystwyth flowing into the sea – the Welsh word 'Aber' actually means 'mouth of the river.' In Belfast, N. Ireland, a stroll by the River Lagan will give you a very welcome respite from the city streets and the so called 'Belfast Buzz.' Most towns then possess rivers, and were established originally because of their proximity to a river, as a river would have supplied vital water supplies for both personal and industrial use.

Were you aware that the Bible both begins and ends with a river? In its opening book we read that *A river flowed out of Eden to water the garden, and there it divided into four rivers*

(Genesis 2:10). Then, in its closing book, John describes the glorious heavenly city so: *Then he showed me the river of the water of life, bright as a crystal, flowing from the throne of God and of the Lamb through the middle of the street of the city* (Revelation 22:1,2).

What exactly is a river? Well if we think about it, it is a large amount of water - much more than a brook or stream - and the water of a river, unlike a lake or a pond, is constantly moving and flowing. A river seldom runs dry, even in the heat of summer, because it is continually replenished either from an underground spring or a stream which runs down the mountains from on high.

With the above paragraph in mind, what a picture a river gives us of the bountiful blessings of Almighty God! His blessings come down from on high. His blessings super abound for all our needs. His blessings are great, abundant and constant, and with God there is more than enough for all, and there will still be more to come and more left over. Let us then look at some of the rivers of the Bible – the Book that begins and ends with a river:-

In Isaiah 43:19,20 God makes the promise *I will make a way in the wilderness and rivers in the desert . . . for I give water in the wilderness and rivers in the desert.* Rivers in the desert! Life and refreshment in the place of deadness and dryness. What volumes this speaks of God's regenerating power. According to the New Testament, a Christian is someone whom God has brought to spiritual life from the deadness and dryness of our trespasses and sins. Have you got this new spiritual life within you? Have you trusted in Jesus and His death on the cross for your sins? If so, you will know the reality behind Paul's words: *the washing of regeneration and renewal which He poured out upon us richly through Jesus Christ our Saviour* (Titus 3:5,6).

In Psalm 46:4 we read: *There is a river whose streams make glad the city of God.* Here we have the river of God's gladness, and it is especially remarkable against the Psalm's background of war, change, turmoil and tumult. The lesson? Even in the midst of adversity and trouble we can still drink of God's river and be glad. On a similar note, in Isaiah 66:12 God promises *I will extend peace to her like a river* (NIV). God's peace is one of the most precious of all His gifts. We have, through Christ, the peace of knowing our sins forgiven - peace with God - but we can also know the peace of God, God's presence, comfort and peace amidst the most trying of circumstances.

Then there is Psalm 36:8 where the Psalmist states of God *Thou givest them drink from the river of Thy delights.* The river of delights. We are reminded that *in Thy presence there is fullness of joy, in Thy right hand are pleasures forever more* (Psalm 16:11). Pleasures forever more! This world's pleasures, you will agree, are most uncertain and unreliable - but God's are not so. Think of the river of His delights. These are eternal pleasures which the world just cannot give or take away.

So there we have a brief walk along the banks of some of the rivers of the Bible: The river of God's generation - life from the dead; the river of God's gladness; the river of God's guardianship and governance and the river of God's goodness and grace - pleasures forever more.

Jesus once went up to the feast of the Tabernacles in Jerusalem. (Interestingly, Jerusalem is one of the few major cities which lacks a river.) At the feast of the Tabernacles it was the custom to pray for rain so that a good harvest was ensured. How fitting then that in that dry and dusty environment Jesus stood up and gave the following invitation – an invitation which still holds true for us today. Jesus said *If anyone thirst, let him come to Me and drink. He who believes in Me, as the Scripture has said, 'Out of his heart shall flow rivers of living water'* (John 7:37).

> See! the streams of living waters
> Springing from eternal love
> Well supply thy sons and daughters
> And all fear of want remove

Who can faint while such a river
Ever flows their thirst to assuage?
Grace which, like the Lord the Giver
Never fails from age to age

Chapter Seven

THE ESSENTIALS OF
THE BIBLE

❖

The story is told of a farmer from the Highlands of Scot-
land who won a trip to the big city of London. It was
quite a shock to him, as he had never been far away from
home before. His reaction on being asked what he thought of
the shops was "Och. I've never seen so many things I can do
without."

Doing without. Seemingly non-essentials can be essential
when you haven't got them! Have you ever forgotten your tooth
brush when going on holiday, for instance, and had difficulty in
procuring another? Have you ever snapped a shoelace at an
inconvenient time? Have you ever not packed a spare pair of
spectacles and lived to regret it? Examples of essential things
taken for granted could no doubt be multiplied.

According to the Bible, there are at least three things which are absolutely essential – we cannot do without them at all. Let us look at these now:-

1. Hebrews 9:22 says *Without the shedding of blood there is no forgiveness of sins.* This refers ultimately to the blood of Jesus, shed on the cross, so that whoever believes in Him, that is, whoever avails themself of the forgiving blood of Jesus, can be assured that their sins are forgiven and that they have peace with God both here and hereafter. The forgiveness of ours sins is essential and integral to salvation, and according to the Bible there is no forgiveness and there never can be any forgiveness apart from the blood of Jesus – His sacrificial death on Calvary's cross. Beware then of a blood-less Christianity. As blood is essential to life, the blood of Jesus is essential to eternal life. We cannot do without it for *without the shedding of blood there is no forgiveness of sins* (Hebrews 9:22).

2. According to the Bible we cannot do without faith. Hebrews 11:6 says *And without faith it is impossible to please Him (God). For whoever would draw near to God must believe that He exists and that He rewards those who seek Him.* Let us repeat that. *Without faith it is impossible to please Him.* Faith, in the biblical sense, means trust or reliance. The *Shorter Catechism* defines it so:'Faith in Jesus Christ is a saving grace whereby we receive and rest upon Him alone for salvation, as He is offered to us in the Gospel.' So we can see why faith is so essential, as apart from faith – personal faith in Jesus Christ and His death on the cross for our sins – His blood avails us nothing. Faith in itself does not save, yet it is definitely the channel though which salvation comes to us. Faith does not save, but faith in Jesus Christ most definitely does. If you have not got this saving faith – *and without faith it is impossible to please Him* – ask God to give it to you. Even the saving faith exercised by us is a gift from God. *By grace you have been saved through faith, and this is not your own doing, it is the gift of God, not because of works, lest any man should boast* (Ephesians 2:8,9).

Faith in Jesus Christ then is a faith that saves. A godly old lady was once asked "Are you the woman with great faith?" She replied "No. I am the woman who has faith in a great God." Absolutely.

3. On a wider level, it is obvious from the Bible that we just cannot do without God Himself. God is the only truly independent and non-dependent being. We are totally dependent, both on each other, but especially upon God. Psalm 127:1 reminds us *Unless the Lord builds the house, those who build it labour in vain.*

A life lived without God is a sorry tale, lacking any meaning, purpose or direction. Whether we acknowledge His existence or not, it is yet true that *In Him we live and move and have our being* (Acts 17:28). The Bible describes Him as *the God in whose hand is your breath* (Daniel 5:23). God is essential. He made us, He sustains us, He provides for us, He comforts us in sorrow, He guides us, He helps us, and most importantly, He saves us when we put our faith in Jesus. The salvation which God gives in Jesus Christ is full-orbed and can be considered negatively, from the penalty and power of sin and also positively, in the sense of restoration to perfect peace and harmony with Himself. *Salvation belongs to our God* (Revelation 7:10) is the Bible's theme.

So then, in this life, I guess that we can do without much. Necessity may force us to view some of our needs as greeds! But we cannot do without the blood of Jesus. We cannot do without faith, and we certainly cannot do without God Himself.

> I need Thee every hour
> Most gracious Lord
> No tender voice like Thine
> Can peace afford
>
> I need Thee, O I need Thee
> Every hour I need Thee
> O bless me now, my Saviour
> I come to Thee

I need Thee every hour
In joy or pain
Come quickly and abide
Or life is vain

I need Thee, O I need Thee
Every hour I need Thee
O bless me now, my Saviour
I come to Thee

Chapter Eight

THE CITIES OF
THE BIBLE

❖

T hose of us who have always lived in a city may some
times envy those who live out in the peace and tranquil-
lity of the countryside. How nice it must be to breathe
fume-free air and live closer to nature, we might think. Reality,
however, can be somewhat different. Those of us who have made
the transfer from city to rural life for a short time, soon long for
former times, after the initial novelty wears off. One person's
quietness is another's eeriness! One person's quaint village life
may soon make another long for 'civilisation' again – a greater
variety of shops, a larger public library, more frequent public trans-
port and the general hustle, bustle and 'life' of living in a big city.

Did you know that the Bible can be viewed as 'The Tale of
Two Cities'? According to the last book of the Bible, Revelation,
our final destination will be one of two cities:- 1. the heavenly

city of the New Jerusalem - the city of those who have been
redeemed by the blood of Christ - whose glory is quite beyond all
that tongue can tell, or 2. the city of Babylon, a city that stands
for all that is opposed to God, even though it has its own political
and religious system which fools and traps many. Needless to
say, this city of Babylon is foretold as coming to a disastrous end:
*Then a mighty angel took up a stone like a great millstone and
threw it into the sea, saying 'So shall Babylon the great city be
thrown down with violence, and shall be found no more. . .'* (Revelation 18:21) along with those described as being *deceived by
its sorcery* (Revelation 18:23). How imperative it is therefore
that we ask ourselves the question 'To which city am I heading
after I die?'

The most famous city in the world must be the city of Jerusalem. Jersualem is held especially dear by both Christians and
Jews alike. The Psalmist esteemed Jersualem so highly that he
went as far to say *If I forget you, O Jerusalem, let my right hand
wither! Let my tongue cleave to the roof of my mouth, if I do not
remember you, if I do not set Jerusalem above my highest joy*
(Psalm 137: 5,6). We cannot read the Bible and avoid Jerusalem.
Jerusalem is mentioned first in the book of Genesis, chapter 14,
in the time of Abraham almost four thousand years ago. Then, as
we have already seen, heaven itself, in the last book of the Bible,
is depicted in terms of a New Jerusalem – the happiest of all
communities, a community of people saved by the grace of God
in Jesus Christ.

A walk around the city walls and ramparts of the old city
of Jerusalem is very much a walk through the scenery of history.
Three thousand years ago king David conquered the city and made
it the religious and political capital of the Jewish nation. But perhaps the most interesting and moving place in Jerusalem is a place
outside its city walls – a place which has permeated Christian
thinking and hymnology for the past two thousand years. You
know the place?:-

There is a green hill far away
without a city wall
Where the dear Lord was crucified
He died to save us all.

Actually the place was not a green hill but a 'skull hill'. But there, outside Jerusalem's city walls is the place where it is believed that Jesus was crucified – the place where, according to prophecy *He was wounded for our transgressions, bruised for our iniquities* (Isaiah 53:5). The earliest Christian creed stated *Christ died for our sins* (1 Corinthians 15:3), and in dying to procure our forgiveness there in the earthly Jerusalem, Jesus removed the barrier of sin for all who believe, so that we may be sure of a place in the heavenly Jerusalem – the Jerusalem which dwarfs its earthly counterpart by infinity.

The Bible relates how Abraham, that archetypal man of faith, *looked forward to the city which has foundations, whose builder and maker is God* (Hebrews 11:10), and the next chapter of Hebrews similarly encourages all Christians by reminding us that *you have come to Mount Zion and to the city of the living God, the heavenly Jerusalem* (Hebrews 11:22). Note that it is *the city of the living God* , as everything which is not of God, be it ever so exciting, seemingly successful or religious, will eventually die. It is good then to 'take inventory' as to whether we are living eternally and for eternal things. The same writer warns us that *here we have no lasting city, but we seek the city which is to come* (Hebrews 13:14). If in doubt then, trust in the One who died outside the walls of Jerusalem for sinners. He is the answer to our alienation and isolation. His death on the cross brings us into fellowship with God and with one another – fellowship now and fellowship in the future, in the city of the living God.

Glorious things of thee are spoken
Zion city of our God
He whose word cannot be broken
Formed thee for His own abode

On the rock of ages founded
What can shake thy sure repose
With salvation's walls surrounded
Thou mayest smile at all thy foes

Saviour, since of Zion's city
I through grace a member am
Let the world deride or pity
I will glory in Thy name
Fading is the worldling's pleasure
All his boasted pomp and show
Solid joys and lasting treasure
None but Zion's children know.

Chapter Nine

THE BALM OF
THE BIBLE

❖

M ost boys, at some stage, have had hopes of being a professional footballer, and most boys, have, at some stage, been stung by the stinging nettles in the local park, whilst retrieving the ball from the bushes during an 'important cup final'. At such uncomfortable times, those who are canny know that the remedy is very near. 'Dock leaves', so called, grow right by stinging nettles. A 'dock leaf', when rubbed on an arm that has been stung, will prove to provide almost instant relief. When the 'dock leaf' is applied, the sting, soreness, redness and swelling will all soon go, enabling play to continue – until either the ball is lost again or mother calls a star player inside for tea.

The Malady of the Sinner

Did you know that death (something we will all have to face sooner or later) has a sting to it? The Bible says *The sting of death is sin, and the power of sin is the law* (1 Corinthians 15:56). Death has a sting to it. Notice that the verse says that death has a sting, not dying, but death itself.

The fear of death is universal. Why? Because human conscience ties in with the teaching of Scripture when it states *It is appointed for men to die once, and after that comes judgement* (Hebrews 9:27). We will all have to stand before God one day and be judged by Him, and there is the sting.

We all know and have known since childhood just how awful it is to have to face someone (such as a parent or a friend) when we have done wrong. If this is so, how much more awful will it be to face an infinitely Holy God, Who sees through us with His all piercing eye, and Who knows just who we really are as well as everything we have ever done whether in public or in private. Yes indeed. *The sting of death is sin.* And the sting is and will be intolerable.

The Remedy of the Saviour

The Christian Faith is God's remedy to take away the sting of death – a 'dock leaf' from heaven, if you like. This dock leaf which takes away the sting of death is none other than God's own Son, the Lord Jesus Christ, and His death on the cross for our sins.

Jesus takes away the sting of death. He did so by actually dying in our place and for our sins and actually taking the full sting of death upon Himself so that we might escape from its barbs. The earliest Christian creed states most concisely: *Christ died for our sins in accordance with the Scriptures* (1 Corinthians 15:3).

Jesus then is heaven's providential remedy. He extracts the sting out of death for all who trust in Him. On the cross, Jesus actually suffered all that we fear the most so that we need never fear. He died for our sins. The Christian can even say 'In my place condemned He stood'. God poured out His holy anger and wrath upon Him when, although sinless Himself, Christ the sinless one accounted for the sinner and paid the dreadful consequence of our sins, so we may go free.

In Jeremiah 8:22 we read: *Is there no balm in Gilead? Is there no physician there? Why then has the health of my people not been restored?* The New Testament answers this with a resounding Yes! There is a balm. It is the blood of Jesus which cleanses us from all sin. So let us quote in full the verses before and after the verse we have been considering and rejoice. Jesus takes away the sting of death. *Death is swallowed up in victory. O death where is thy victory? O death, where is thy sting? The sting of death is sin, and the power of sin is the law. But thanks be to God, Who gives us the victory through our Lord Jesus Christ* (1 Corinthians 15:55,56).

> We sing the praise of Him who died
> Of Him who died upon the cross;
> The sinner's hope let men deride,
> For this we count the world but loss.
>
> The cross! it takes our guilt away;
> It holds the fainting spirit up;
> It cheers with hope the gloomy day,
> And sweetens every bitter cup.
>
> *The balm of life,* the cure of woe,
> The measure and the pledge of love,
> The sinner's refuge here below,
> The angels' theme in heaven above.

Chapter Ten

THE CLOTHES OF
THE BIBLE

❖

C lothes can be a touchy subject, especially with teenagers. What a teenager says is 'in' is often 'out' with their parents and vice versa. Interestingly, C. H. Spurgeon once said "There is nothing as out of date as the latest fashion." When we see pictures of the long hair, flaired trousers and platform soles which were in vogue in the 1970's, we may be inclined to agree.

The clothing of the Bible is fascinating. The first mention of clothes is back in the garden of Eden. No sooner had sin and shame entered the scene when God stepped in, in mercy, for we read *the Lord God made for Adam and for his wife garments of skins and clothed them* (Genesis 3:21).

Clothing is both functional and fashionable. Whilst worn on the outside, they can reveal something of what a person is like on the inside. This being so, let us consider:-

1. The Garments of Sin

Isaiah 64:6 reads *We have all become like one who is unclean, and all our righteous deeds are like a polluted garment.* We thus need a change of clothing if we are going to be fit for God's presence – and this needed change of clothing is provided for us in the Gospel. Zechariah 3:3,4 pictures this for us: *Joshua was standing before the angel clothed with filthy garments. And the angel said to those who were standing before him "Remove the filthy garments from him." And to him he said, "Behold, I have taken away your iniquity from you, and I will clothe you with rich apparel."*

2. The Garments of the Saviour

In Luke 8:47,48 we read *A woman who had a flow of blood for twelve years and could not be healed by any one, came up behind Him, (Jesus), and touched the fringe of His garment; immediately her flow of blood ceased.* The garment in question here was the tassel. As an obedient Jew, Jesus would have obeyed Deuteronomy 22:12: *You shall make yourself tassels on the four corners of your cloak with which to cover yourself.* A touch of this garment on this Person though transformed this poor woman's life. Her illness was such that she would have been defiled, destitute, discouraged and desperate; but one touch of Jesus's garment brought instant deliverance and delight! The tassel of the Lord Jesus therefore teaches us that He is both a touchable and a transforming Saviour.

> Oh touch the hem of His garment
> and thou too shalt be free
> His saving power this very hour
> shall give new life to thee.

3. The Garments of Service

At the very first Lord's Supper in John 13, we read that *Jesus . . . rose from supper, laid aside His garments, and girded Himself with a towel. Then He poured water into a basin and began to wash His disciples' feet, and to wipe them with the towel with which He was girded* (John 13:4,5). What staggering humility! Jesus is the eternal Son of God – 'Christ by highest heaven adored' – but here we see Him washing the disciples' feet, a task assigned to the lowest of slaves. *Though He was in the form of God . . . (He) emptied Himself, taking the form of a servant . . .* (Philippians 2:6,7). In this we have both an expiation and an example. An expiation because Jesus washes our guilt away. An example because we are to emulate the spirit of His action. *If I then, your Lord and Teacher, have washed your feet, you also ought to wash one another's feet* (John 13:14).

4. The Garments of Sacrifice

At the cross, in fulfilment of Psalm 22:18, we read *When the soldiers had crucified Jesus they took His garments and made four parts, one for each soldier; also His tunic. But the tunic was without seam, woven from top to bottom; so they said to one another, "Let us not tear it, but cast lots for it to see whose it shall be"* (John 19:23,24). This seamless robe of Jesus speaks of the sinless life of Jesus – a life laid down in sacrifice. On the cross, Jesus' seamless robe was taken from Him and our filthy rags were put upon Him for *He Himself bore our sins in His body on the tree* (1 Peter 2:24). On the cross a change of clothing occurred when *For our sake He made Him to be sin who knew no sin so that in Him we might become the righteousness of God* (2 Corinthians 5:21). Which leads us to:-

5. The Garments of Salvation

Isaiah 61:10 reads *I will greatly rejoice in the Lord, my soul shall exult in my God; for He has clothed me with the garments of salvation; He has covered me with the robe of righteousness.* The garments of salvation? Surely this refers to the imputed righteousness of Christ – the sinlessness of Christ which avails for guilty sinners and clothes us with a righteousness which fits us for heaven – amongst the *great multitude which no man can number . . . clothed in white robes* (Revelation 7:9).

> Jesus, Thy blood and righteousness,
> My beauty are my glorious dress
> 'Midst flaming worlds in these arrayed,
> With joy shall I lift up my head
>
> This spotless robe the same appears
> When ruined nature sinks in years
> No age can change its glorious hue,
> The robe of Christ is ever new.

Chapter Eleven

THE HONEY OF
THE BIBLE

❖

H ere is an unusual verse. At the end of Psalm 81 God makes
the assertion: *with honey from the rock I would satisfy
you* (Psalm 81:16). Honey from the rock? That's quite a
paradox, as rock is one of the hardest of substances, whilst honey
is one of nature's sweetest. Here then, God says that He will bring
sweetness out of hardness, or, if you like, the nice out of the nasty.

One commentator, speaking on the literal background to
this verse against its middle-eastern setting wrote: 'The countless fissures and crevices of the dry limestone rocks supported
many small flowering plants well suited to the needs of bees.'
Earlier on in the Old Testament God had supplied needed water
from a rock (Exodus 17:6 et al). In God's provision of *honey
from the rock* we see how His goodness is neither exhausted nor
limited by even the best He has given in the past.

Honey from the rock. - the sweet from the hard. Can it really be true? Yes it can! To prove it, consider it from three particular angles:-

1. Christ's Experience

The hardest experience that the Lord Jesus ever faced was without a doubt His death on the cross. This entailed His being betrayed by a friend, slandered by His enemies, generally humiliated and nailed to a plank of wood and hung up to die in the midst of a public thoroughfare. It was an indescribable agony – and yet it resulted in great sweetness. Christ's cruel cross was not in vain. He died in the place of sinners, shedding His precious blood so that all who believe in Him can know and enjoy God's forgiveness. His death resulted in great sweetness – eternal life for all who trust in Him. It was prophesied of Jesus *He shall see the fruit of the travail of His soul and be satisfied* (Isaiah 53:11). The imagery here is that of childbirth. Childbirth is a process of great pain, but from it results the joy of a new life. Similarly, the pain of Calvary results in the joy of new life for all who believe – and this life is eternal! Christ's experience certainly was a case of sweetness from hardness or, *honey from the rock..*

2. Conversion Experience

There is surely no earthly experience sweeter than conversion. Conversion means turning to God, trusting in Jesus and experiencing His abundant love, mercy, grace and forgiveness. Conversion is God's work in us and on us. We cannot and could never convert ourselves. Only Almighty God can bring spiritual life to the spiritually dead. Conversion is so sweet. It is honey – and yet it is *honey from the rock.* Why? Because conviction of sin always precedes conversion. Human guilt always precedes divine grace. Before we can be saved we have to realise - or by

God's grace, be made to realise - that we are sinners in desperate need of a Saviour. Before we can go to heaven we have to realise that apart from Jesus we are on the road to hell. It is a hard experience, but God brings us down to lift us up. He breaks us and then remakes us. Sorrow for sin leads to the joy of God's salvation. Conversion experience also then is *honey from the rock.*

3. Christian Experience

If you are already a Christian, you will know that the Christian life can be very rough at times. In His superior love and infinite wisdom, God sees fit to weave trials, difficulties and even heartaches into every Christian life. They are hard experiences and yet great sweetness results from them, just as a fragrant flower exudes the sweetest of perfumes when it is crushed.

C. S. Lewis once wrote: 'God whispers to us in our pleasures, speaks to us in our consciences but shouts to us in our pain. It is His megaphone for rousing a deaf world.'

Amazingly, our faith and trust in God can be deepened and strengthened by the hard experiences of life. When all is well and smooth, how easy it is to stray from God. But come some trouble, how we are drawn closer to Him, and how much more real and earnest do our prayers become.

When through the deep waters I cause thee to go
The rivers of woe shall not thee overflow
For I will be with thee, thy troubles to bless
And sanctify to thee thy deepest distress

When through fiery trials thy pathway shall lie
My grace all-sufficient shall be thy supply
The flame shall not hurt thee: I only design
Thy dross to consume, and thy gold to refine

Finally though, what about the hardest experience of all? What about death? According to the Bible, death is *the last enemy* (1 Corinthians 15:26). Yet death, for the Christian will be the ultimate experience of *honey from the rock*, for it is in dying that we will inherit eternal life – that eternal home in heaven with the One who loved us and gave Himself for us. The pain of death will lead to the Paradise of God. Faith then will be turned into sight, and we will be free from all the hard rocks of this world, and enjoy the honey of God's presence for all eternity.

God therefore promises: *with honey from the rock I would satisfy you.*

O taste and see that the Lord is good! Happy is the man who takes refuge in Him (Psalm 34:8).

Chapter Twelve

THE SNOWS OF
THE BIBLE

❖

The first snow in winter always seems to come as some thing of a surprise. Children always greet it with delight, especially if it means a day off school. Snowmen and toboggans can be infinitely preferable to mental arithmetic. Even those of more mature years though, when pressed, would probably admit to enjoying walking in virgin snow – making tracks and treading where no one has trodden before. Not everyone though appreciates the snow. It can be rather inconvenient. There is the danger of slipping and injuring yourself; for the elderly it can give a not too nice feeling of being house bound and cut off. Then what of burst pipes? Also, in a few days time the lovely whiteness outside will no doubt be replaced by an unpicturesque muddy, gritty slush.

In the Bible, snow is used to depict three great fundamental truths – truths which affect us all. The snows depicted are:-

1. The Snow of Peerless Splendour 2. The Snow of Pitiful Sinners and 3. The Snow of Perfect Salvation.

1. The Snow of Peerless Splendour

The Bible declares that *God is light and in Him is no darkness at all* (1 John 1:5). This refers to the awesome purity of God in His essence – a purity that is beyond our wildest conception. Daniel, in his vision of God, described Him in the best way our limited vocabulary can, in saying *His raiment was white as <u>snow</u> and His head like pure wool* (Daniel 7:9). Then, in the last book of the Bible John literally fell over when he glimpsed the Lord Jesus in all His glory as *His head and hair were white as white wool, <u>white as snow;</u> His eyes were like a flame of fire* (Revelation 1:14).

Here our dilemma begins. We are all made to know and love God, but when we sense His dazzling splendour and holiness, we understandably shrink back and hide. Which leads us to:-

2. The Snow of Pitiful Sinners

Snow can look so lovely. On some days we may even consider that the view from our windows would almost grace a picture postcard. But if we were to dig below the surface, what would we find? Alas dirt, soil and rubbish . . . Isn't that just like us? We may of course hide and cover our inner selves and fool people, but our rotten inside is not hidden from God. The Bible says *The Lord sees not as man sees; man looks on the outward appearance, but the Lord looks on the heart* (1 Samuel 16:7).

The state of our hearts is such that we are unfit for fellowship with a holy God. And when we realise this, we can use the words of the Psalmist who, if you please, having lapsed into adultery, and suffering the pangs of conscience accordingly, cried out to God. Realising the pollution of his innermost being he prayed *Create in me a clean heart O God . . . Purge me with hyssop and I shall be clean, wash me and I shall be whiter than snow* (Psalm 51:7). It is sad but true. Our outward covering of snow cannot cover up the sin which lies beneath the surface. The good news is though that the Bible reveals that there is:-

3. The Snow of Perfect Salvation

The longest book in the Bible is the prophecy of Isaiah, a formidable sixty six chapters. Isaiah opens his book describing the sorry state of the nation of Israel – and by implication our sorry state: *Ah sinful nation, a people laden with iniquity , offspring of evildoers* (Isaiah 1:4). But a few verses later, God gives this wonderful promise – a promise of perfect salvation: *Come now, let us reason together, says the Lord: though your sins are like scarlet, they shall be as white as snow; though they are red like crimson, they shall become like wool.*

Can it really be true? Is there a way in which our 'insides' can be cleansed? The Bible says that there is. And this is the Christian Good News - the Gospel.

The Bible declares that *The blood of Jesus His Son cleanses us from all sin* (1 John 1:7). We may not fully understand it, but with countless others we may know that it is true.

The last book of the Bible describes the inhabitants of heaven. These people are not necessarily good people, as in God's sight none are good. But they are cleansed people, as we read of them *they have washed their robes and made them white in the blood of the Lamb* (Revelation 7:14).

So there it is. Do you believe it? There may be many things which we do not understand - electricity and word processors, for example - yet we can still use them and appreciate their benefits. Similarly, we may not understand how Jesus' blood cleanses

us from sin and makes us fit for heaven, but this need not keep us
from enjoying and benefiting from its infinite blessings.

Would you be whiter, much whiter than snow?
There's power in the blood, power in the blood
Sin stains are lost in its life giving flow
There's wonderful power in the blood

There is power, power, wonder working power
in the precious blood of the Lamb.

Chapter Thirteen

THE CLOUDS OF
THE BIBLE

❖

We British, living on an island of unpredictable weather, often find ourselves being keen observers of the clouds. Many of us have memories of family picnics in the summer. The picnic is just ready, we are revelling in the sun and clear blues skies . . . and then the clouds roll up and send us dashing for cover as the first drops of rain come down. Then there are the more formal occasions such as a fete, garden party or perhaps even a wedding. Serious faces keep looking at the clouds, hoping that they will blow over.

Clouds. I notice that clouds feature quite often in the Bible, usually at momentous times in history. This being so, let us look at some of them:-

The Cloud of God

When God gave the Ten Commandments at Mount Sinai, we read that there was *a thick cloud upon the mountain . . . so that all the people who were in the camp trembled* (Exodus 19:16). The cloud here symbolised the visible presence of the invisible God Himself. It was a formidable occasion and no wonder that the people trembled. It reminds us that God demands our utmost respect, reverence and worship.

Similarly, when the Temple was built in Jerusalem a few centuries later in the time of King Solomon, something of God's awesome presence was there too – symbolised by a cloud. *A cloud filled the house of the Lord, so that the priests could not stand to minister because of the cloud, for the glory of the Lord filled the house of the Lord* (1 Kings 8:10,11).

The Cloud of God's Guidance

The Israelites were guided by God by a cloud when they wandered through the wilderness. *In the daytime He led them with a cloud* (Psalm 78:14). We may apply this to ourselves. Are you perplexed and in need of guidance? Are you unsure which way to turn? Well, ask the Lord God. He is the Lord of our circumstances and exercises sovereign control over all things, great and small. He is infinite in wisdom and knows the end from the beginning. He has promised us in His Word: *I will instruct you and teach you the way you should go; I will counsel you with my eye upon you* (Psalm 32:8).

The Cloud of God's Generosity

Clouds, in the Bible, actually speak of God's goodness and generosity – even of His blessing. No clouds mean no rain, and no rain was and still is a serious matter in the land of the Bible. Clouds therefore speak of the bounty of the God Who *covers the heavens with clouds, . . . prepares rain for the earth, and makes grass grow upon the hills* (Psalm 147:8). The clouds of God's blessing. How easy it is to get bowed down with our trials and tribulations. How good it would be if, inspite of them we could yet sing 'Count your many blessings, name them one by one, and it will surprise you what the Lord your God has done.'

The Cloud of God's Greatness

When we turn to the New Testament we see that clouds also feature in the life of Jesus. We think, for instance of that amazing time in Jesus' life known as the Transfiguration, when something of Jesus' pre-incarnate glory broke through. There, on that high mountain, amongst other things *a cloud overshadowed them, and a voice came out of the cloud, 'This is My beloved Son; listen to Him'* (Mark 9:7). The cloud certainly gives us a glimpse of Jesus's surpassing and superlative greatness.

The Cloud of God's Golgotha

Golgotha was the most awesome moment in all history. At Golgotha Jesus died on a cross bearing our sins and God's judgement upon them so that we might go free when we trust in Him. Golgotha was a time of supernatural darkness. Sin is a black affair, and Jesus took God's wrath on our sins in full. Small wonder that creation itself shuddered. *There was darkness over the whole earth* (Mark 15:33). Perhaps it was a cloud that blocked out the light of the midday sun here, at this most important event in all history .

The Cloud of God's Glory

Finally, the Bible reveals that clouds are going to feature in an event still future. Jesus is coming again – the Bible says so no less than 318 times. What will that day be like? Well Jesus said *they will see the Son of Man coming in clouds with great power and glory* (Mark 13:26) and John foretold *Behold, He is coming with the clouds* (Revelation 1:7). What a day that will be, when Jesus comes to reign and bring in His everlasting kingdom of righteousness and peace. Are you ready for that day?

So there are some of the clouds of the Bible. Someone reading this though might be thinking of some other cloud. When we experience unhappiness in this life we often say that it is as if a big black cloud is hanging over us. Perhaps you may be feeling 'under a cloud' at the moment.

The Cloud of God's Groaners

Man is born to trouble as the sparks fly upward (Job 5:7). And Christians are certainly not exempt from black clouds, even if the majority have a 'silver lining'. Whatever cloud you or I may be under though, we both have access to God through Christ by prayer. So 'take it to the Lord in prayer.' He understands. He knows. He can help you like no one else can. Jesus is able to lift the blackest of clouds, for 'burdens are lifted at Calvary, Jesus is very near.'

There was once a hymn writer who also knew dreadful trials. Out of them he was able to write the following lines. On these I'll close our thoughts on the clouds of the Bible:-

You fearful saints, fresh courage take
The *clouds* that you so dread
Are big with mercy and will break
In blessings on your head

Judge not the Lord by feeble sense
But trust Him for His grace
Behind a frowning providence
He hides a smiling face.

Chapter Fourteen

THE SUNSHINE OF
THE BIBLE

❖

I t is sad when we find out that the things we enjoy may be bad
for us. Such has fairly recently become the case with sunshine. These days, in the summer, we are warned not to sit in
the sun for too long as it may cause skin cancer. Thus beach
inspectors, weather men, skin specialists and the makers of
the various sun-bloc creams variously do their best to put a brake
on our enjoyment and not over indulge. *Light is sweet, and
it is pleasant for the eyes to behold the sun* (Ecclesiastes 11:7),
wrote Koheleth – but the ozone layer was not so thin in his
day!

Interestingly, the Bible has something to say about the sun.
It actually mentions it on the very first page where we read that
*God made the two great lights, the greater light to rule the day
and the lesser light to rule the night* (Genesis 1:16). Then Psalm

84:11 reads *For the Lord God is a sun and shield, He bestows favour and honour* and in the very last chapter of the Old Testament we read of the promise that *the sun of righteousness shall rise, with healing in its wings* (Malachi 4:2).

The sun of righteousness shall rise with healing in its wings. Christians have traditionally taken this final Old Testament prophecy as referring to none less than the Lord Jesus Christ and so the title has crept into some of our hymns. The famous Christmas hymn 'Hark the herald angels sing,' for instance, includes the stanza of praise to Jesus:-

> Hail Thou heaven-born prince of peace
> Hail Thou *Sun of Righteousness*
> Light and life to all He brings
> Risen with healing in His wings

The sun is absolutely vital for life. If the sun should cease, then life itself would cease, as all plant and animal life would die out. Jesus is similarly essential for spiritual life. The Bible is clear. There is no spiritual life apart from a faith-union with Jesus Christ. John 1:4 says of Jesus *In Him was life, and the life was the light of men.* Jesus then is the eternally living Son of God, our life and light giving Saviour for us who by nature are born both spiritually dead and in spiritual darkness. How we need the life and light He imparts!

Notice that Malachi promised *the Sun of Righteousness shall rise with healing in its wings.* The sun is associated with healing and health. Sufferers from bad backs often have treatment with a sun lamp. Sun lamp treatment can ease aching muscles and even certain forms of seasonal depression. The cure for the latter involves the patient sitting in a room under a lamp which simulates sunshine. Jesus, the *Sun of Righteousness* brings healing. He is the One Who heals our broken relationship with God. Our sin has broken our relationship with God, but on the cross Jesus took our sins upon Himself, so breaking down the sin barrier between ourselves and our Maker. He is the *Sun of Righteousness.* To be technical, He 'imputes' His righteousness to the believer, putting us right with God, bringing us spiritual healing and harmony. This is a constant source of Christian joy. The ancients loved the sun. As we have seen, they agreed that *Light is sweet and it is pleasant for the eyes to behold the sun.* How much more sweet and pleasant though is the everlasting Christian joy. Romans 5:11: *we . . . rejoice in God through our Lord Jesus Christ, through whom we have now received our reconciliation.*

Finally, and this is not so agreeable, we are all aware that the sun can be destructive as well as delightful. It can burn us as well as bless us. The same sun which causes a sun-tan can also cause a forest fire. The sun, in the Bible, is also used to describe the awful judgement which awaits all those who reject God's offer of mercy in Jesus Christ. Revelation 16:8 is fearful reading. It may well be symbolic, but the question is, symbolic of what? Listen to what it says: *The fourth angel poured his bowl on the sun, and it was allowed to scorch men with fire; men were scorched by the fierce heat, and they cursed the name of God who had power over these plagues, and they did not repent and give Him glory.*

Yes, a fearful fate awaits those who reject Jesus, *the Sun of Righteousness.* The same sun which melts the wax can also harden the clay. The same sun which brings life, light and healing and health can also bring the most fearsome destruction. It is vital that we trust in Jesus as our own personal Saviour therefore. He promised *Truly truly I say to you, he who hears my Word and believes Him who sent me has eternal life; he does not come into judgement but has passed from death to life* (John 5:24).

There can be no better way of concluding this brief meditation on God's sunshine than by using the Old Testament blessing which goes like this:-

The Lord bless you and keep you
The Lord make His face to shine upon you, and be gracious to
you
The Lord lift up His countenance upon you and give you peace
(Numbers 6:24-26).

Chapter Fifteen

THE SEAS OF
THE BIBLE

❖

"Oh . . . I . . . *do* like to be beside the seaside . . ." And we British, being an island people, certainly do. Some of us are priviliged to live a mere five minutes from the sea front, and can highly recommend living by the sea. The novelty never quite wears off. A stroll along the prom. is the ideal way to blow the cobwebs out of the lungs. It is good too to be able to observe the sea in all its different moods from the lake-like calm of the summer to the quite violent winter storms. Especially thrilling is being able to go for an evening bracer on the sea front - the squawking gulls, the smell of ozone, the regular, rhythmic crashing of the waves upon the shore, the sun sinking into the horizon . . . There's nothing like it.

The sea is mentioned many times in the Bible in various contexts. Let us consider some of these now:-

First of all, the vast awesomeness of the sea tells us something about God the creator. The Bible states *The sea is His for He made it* (Psalm 95:5). Whilst the immensity of the sea 'drowns' us into insignificance and makes us feel very small, not so with God. Isaiah tells us that God *has measured the waters in the hollow of His hand* (Isaiah 40:12). So talk about having a Friend with power! If you know God, you know the ultimate power and authority, as He Who created the sea also made you and knows what is best for you. At your request He will even use His power and love to help you.

Secondly, the sea in the Bible also teaches us something about God as ruler. How helpless we feel when the sea storms rage – we are powerless against such a frightening force. But the Bible says of God: *Thou dost rule the raging of the sea; when its waves rise, Thou stillest them* (Psalm 89:9) and that *Mightier than the thunders of many waters, mightier than the waves of the sea, the Lord on high is mighty* (Psalm 93:4). What a comfort this is when we face the storms of life – and storms are certain to come to us at some time or other. How do you react when the waves beat and crash against your heart's door? Remember the time when Jesus demonstrated His total Lordship over nature when He stilled the stormy Sea of Galilee (see Mark 4:35-41). How relieved were His petrified disciples at that time. Of course, Jesus may not see fit to take away our personal storms immediately, but if we ask Him, He will certainly be with us and give us the strength to cope with whatever difficulty we find ourselves in. Many can even say that it was at a time of crisis that they either first came to know God, or their faith in Him was deepened as they proved His faithfulness more. A phrase says 'Man's extremity is God's opportunity.' The Bible assures us that *God is our refuge and strength, a very present help in time of trouble* (Psalm 46:1).

Thirdly, the sea in the Bible pictures something of the infinite forgiveness of God to the sinner who trusts in Him. The same prophet who predicted Jesus's birth in Bethlehem drew His prophesy to a close with the words *Thou will cast all our sins into the depths of the sea* (Micah 7:19). Imagine that! God's forgiveness is as vast and immeasurable as the wide wide ocean. All our sins - the sins which would keep us out of heaven if left unforgiven - can be buried in the depths of the sea, forgiven and forgotten for ever. The Christian knows that the prophet was speaking about Jesus here. On the cross, Jesus paid the penalty for our sins. Therefore through Jesus, God is able justly both to forgive and forget all of our sins. This truly is a salvation that this world cannot offer.

Lastly, according to the Bible, one day the sea will be no more. With prophetic foresight John saw that the *sea was no more* (Revelation 21:1). If we are fond of the sea, we may at first be a little sad to be told that one day our beloved sea will be gone for ever.   With a little research though we realise that in the Bible, the sea is also a picture of wickedness – something we can well do without. The sea, as we all know, has some frightening, dangerous aspects to it – just as evil is frightening, dangerous and destructive. The Bible states that *the wicked are like the tossing sea; for it cannot rest, and its waters toss up mire and dirt . There is no peace, says my God, for the wicked* (Isaiah 57:20). So it is good to know that one day there is the certain prospect that God, in His good time, will totally eradicate all the evil and frightening aspects of this world. More, He will destroy all evil and bring in His promised *new heavens and a new earth in which righteousness dwells* (2 Peter 3:13).

Oh the deep deep love of Jesus
Vast, unmeasured, boundless free
Rolling as a mighty ocean
In its fullness over me
Underneath me, all around me
Is the current of Thy love
Leading onward, leading homeward
To my glorious home above.

Chapter Sixteen

THE HIGHEST BLESSING
OF THE BIBLE

❖

Proverbs 10:22 reads *The blessing of the Lord makes rich, and He adds no sorrow with it.* Surely, there is not one person on earth who does not want to be happy, and it is the Bible, and the Bible alone which shows us how we can be truly happy, that is truly blessed. The Bible reveals to us the great Gospel blessings and privileges which are ours if we believe in Jesus, and these blessings are numerous. Think of the blessing of divine forgiveness – because of the cross, God is able to justly forgive and erase all our sins, giving us a clean sheet and a new start. Think of the blessing of divine justification – God's justification means that, because of the cross, He is able to declare us 'Not guilty', for in Christ we are for ever acquitted and free from condemnation. Think of the blessing of redemption – Christ's death on the cross frees us from the penalty, power and one day the very presence of sin. Then there are the blessings of, for example, eternal life, propitiation, reconciliation, true hope and a home in heaven with God by and by. The blessings which flow from God - 'the fount of every blessing' are innumerable. It is good that we will have eternity in which to praise Him because we will need it!

What, however, do you think is the Christian's highest blessing and privilege? With no hesitation, it must be the blessing of adoption. Adoption. And it is the wonder of divine adoption - a wonder almost too good to be true - that I should like us to consider now.

What then is adoption? *The Shorter Catechism* gives a concise definition thus: 'Adoption is an act of God's free grace, whereby we are received into the number, and have a right to all the privileges of the sons of God.'

Adoption refers to the change of our standing and status by God and before God. Through Christ, He changes us from being children of wrath to being children of God. He literally brings us into His family, so that we can call Him 'Our Father' and enjoy living under His authority, affection and fatherly care, totally secure. Adoption means that we have the most wonderful privileges now here in this world – but adoption also means that we are heirs of the most wonderful inheritance in the next world too, for one day we will inherit all of God's glories and treasures in a way that words just cannot describe - *if children then heirs, heirs of God and fellow heirs with Christ* (Romans 8:17).

Let us see some of the New Testament Scriptures which speak of adoption then. Note well that the Bible teaches that all are not automatically children of God by birth. No. Whilst God is the Father of us all by virtue of His creating us, He is the real Father only of those who have been adopted into His family through Jesus. Jesus is *the* Son of God. We become sons or children of God through Him, and through Him alone:-

John wrote: *to all who received Him (Jesus), who believed in His name, He gave power to become children of God; who were born, not of blood nor of the will of the flesh nor of the will of man, but of God* (John 1:12,13).

Paul wrote: *in Christ Jesus you are all sons of God through faith* (Galatians 3:26). *God sent forth His Son . . . that we might receive adoption as sons. And because you are sons, God has sent the Spirit of His Son into our hearts crying 'Abba! Father!' So through God you are no longer a slave but a son, and if a son then an heir* (Galatians 4:5,6).

What a difference there is between being someone's servant, someone's friend and someone's son. The crucial question is then, do you know for sure that you are a child of God? Have you that intimate, endearing relationship with God, just like a father and a child? This can be yours if you trust in Jesus, God's Son. And once it is yours, it is yours for time and eternity, for God will never cast His children out (see John 6:37). If it is not yours however, according to the Bible, you will be separated from God and under His displeasure for all eternity (cf Matthew 7:23 and 25:41).

God adopts sinners. It is a staggering truth. Sinners have an infinite change of status when they 'come to the Father through Jesus the Son.' On the cross Jesus took all of God's anger against our sins so that we could be adopted into God's family. It is a costly adoption – an adoption through the propitiation of the cross.

If, however, you have been a Christian for many years, be careful not to let the wonder of who you are grow stale. The freshness of faith of the apostle John comes sometimes as a rebuke. John, even though now an old man, could still exclaim: *See what love the Father has given us, that we should be called children of God; and so we are* (1 John 3:1). Can we?

If you are a Christian, you are a child of the King of kings. You will not want to change places with anyone. Why step down to become a millionaire?

O how shall I the goodness tell
Father, which Thou to me hast showed?
That I, a child of wrath and hell
I should be called a child of God
Should know, should feel my sins forgiven
Blest with this antepast of heaven.

(For the doctrine of adoption in greater detail, see chapter 3 of the author's *Comfort From The Bible: Help For Those Who Hurt*, Belfast, 1996).

Chapter Seventeen

THE KISSES OF
THE BIBLE

❖

One of the most heart-breaking experiences anyone can have is that of kissing a loved one goodbye, knowing that it will be a long time before the next meeting. The dictionary defines a kiss as 'to touch with the lips as a sign of affection, reverence etc.' When you analyse it, it is a strange way of showing affection – yet we all do it. We wonder how and why the practice originated. Perhaps a visit to the anthropology section of a town library sometime would give us some clues.

In this chapter I should like to give you three kisses! Not quite. Rather I should like to draw your attention to three kisses in the Bible and see what they have to say to us:-

1. The Kiss of Deliverance

Our first kiss may be found in Psalm 2:11,12 which reads:-

Serve the Lord with fear, with trembling <u>kiss</u> His feet, lest He be angry and you perish in the way, for His wrath is quickly kindled. Blessed are all who take refuge in Him.

The message of this kiss is simple but solemn. Either we submit to God now and make friends with Him through His Son Jesus Christ, or one day we will have to bow before God as our Judge, Whose anger will be upon us for ever. This in turn begs some crucial questions: Have I bowed the knee to God? Have I admitted that He is the King of kings and Lord of lords? Have I confessed that I am a sinner? Have I begged Him to have mercy upon me?

2. The Kiss of Devotion

The second kiss may be found in Luke chapter 7. There we read of a woman of quite ill-repute who:-*brought an alabaster flask of ointment, and standing behind (Jesus) at His feet, weeping, she began to wet His feet with her tears, and wiped them with the hair of her head, and <u>kissed</u> His feet, and anointed them with the ointment.*

Strange? But Jesus gave the explanation for her behaviour:-
She has not ceased to kiss My feet . . . Therefore I tell you, her sins, which are many, are forgiven, for she loved much; but he who is forgiven little loves little.

Do you see the point? Our devotion to Jesus - symbolised here by literally kissing His feet - will only happen if we realise just how much He loves us and just how much He has forgiven us and just how great was the price He paid for our forgiveness when He shed His life blood on the cross. Are we then devoted to Jesus shamelessly, like that un-named woman? If our first love for Him has gone cold, we must remind ourselves of just how much He loves us. If however you know nothing of the love of God in Christ at all, pray to God that He will reveal His love in Christ to you. When He does you will only be able to respond with love, praise and devotion. Devotion never just happens. It is always an intelligent response to God's first love towards us, undeserving and ill deserving though we are. *We love, because He first loved us* (1 John 4:19).

3. The Kiss of Damnation

Finally, what about this kiss - perhaps the most infamous kiss of all. What about the kiss of Judas Iscariot? Judas was a disciple of Jesus for three whole years, but has gone down in history as the man who betrayed Jesus with a kiss. Humanly speaking, how must Jesus have felt at being on the receiving end of such an evil act? *'Judas, would you betray the Son of Man with a kiss?'* (Luke 22:48). No one gives their son the name Judas. Judas Iscariot is an enigmatic figure. He was fully responsible for what he did, even though it was all predestined by God to take place. He came to a very sad end. He committed suicide in a field known as 'Akeldama' *the Field of Blood* (Matthew 27:8). To stand near to the the site of Akeldama, which is still in Jerusalem, is a sobering, shuddering experience . Judas is now in hell, even though during Jesus' ministry he seemed to be a genuine disciple. Such an eternity in hell is the lot of all who reject Jesus. Rejection of Jesus means a rejection of God's mercy, and rejection of God's mercy means an eternity in hell. God's mercy to the sinner reached its pinnacle on the cross where, with prophetic foresight the Psalmist wrote *Steadfast love and faithfulness met, righteousness and peace kissed each other* (Psalm 85:10).

So ask yourself the question 'In which category am I?' Have I bowed the knee to God and, metaphorically speaking, 'kissed His feet'? Am I devoted to the Jesus Who died to procure my forgiveness? Or am I like Judas, the man who betrayed His Master with a kiss and came to an irreparable doom?

Chapter Eighteen

THE FOOLS OF
THE BIBLE

❖

pril Fool's Day, so called, has many hazards. It seems to
bring out the mischief in many otherwise sane and
sensible adults. Zoos, we are told, are plagued by calls
asking for a Mr Lion on that day. Then there was the lady who
fooled her husband into thinking that they had won the National
Lottery. He was convinced that he was a multi-millionaire, but
did not find it at all funny when he found out that he had been
hoaxed. In olden days some people were employed as professional fools or court jesters. Whilst long gone, their ghosts seem
to reappear each April 1st.

In this chapter I should like us to consider the subject of
the fools of the Bible. In 1 Samuel 26:21 King Saul said *I have
played the fool and erred exceedingly.* Saul started off well, but
went off the rails. He disobeyed God and came to a very nasty
end – as indeed do all who are not on God's side.

The three biblical fools I should like us to consider now are 1. The Atheist 2. The Materialist and 3. The Evangelist.

1. The Atheist

In both Psalm 14:1 and 53:1 we read *The fool says in his heart "There is no God."* Atheists then, that is, those who try to deny God's very existence, are fools. The author knows of one professing atheist who even asked for an atheistic funeral when he died. He is dead now and his wishes were granted. What a fool. He knows now that God exists, only it is now too late. Interestingly, the Bible never gives any reasons or arguments for the existence of God. It just assumes it. The evidence for it is so compelling that it takes it for granted – just as we do not go around proving that our friends exist.

C. H. Spurgeon said of our fool in question:-

The atheist is the fool pre-eminently, and a fool universally. . . Sin is always folly. As it is the height of sin to attack the very existence of the Most High, so is it also the greatest imaginable folly. To say there is no God is to belie the plainest evidence, which is obstinacy; to oppose the common consent of mankind, which is stupidity; to stifle consciousness, which is madness . . . But as denying the existence of fire does not prevent its burning a man who is in it, so doubting the existence of God will not stop the Judge of all the earth from destroying the rebel who breaks His laws . . .

The atheist then, according to the Bible, is an utter fool, but so also is:-

2. The Materialist

In Luke 12:16 ff., Jesus tells a parable of a rich fool. He told how *The land of a rich man brought forth plentifully; and he thought to himself "What shall I do for I have nowhere to store my crops?" And he said, "I will do this: I will pull down my barns, and build larger ones; and there I will store all my grain and my goods. And I will say to my soul, Soul, you have ample goods laid up for many years; take your ease, eat, drink and be merry." But God said to him, "Fool! This night your soul is required of you; and the things you have prepared, whose will they be?"* The foolish materialist. He was rich in goods but poor in soul. He was more interested in money than mercy, in gold rather than God. He was prepared for this life but not for the next. His vision was limited to the earthly and material until, to his great shock, God took his life away, and he had to reckon with the spiritual and the eternal. The rich fool lived without God and then died without God. Eternally, his wealth counted for nothing at all. There is surely a lesson for us too here. We too should beware of the dangers of riches. Finally, and more happily, consider

3. The Evangelist

We are fools for Christ's sake (1 Corinthians 4:10) wrote Paul. For Paul, Christ was the reason for living. He wrote elsewhere *For me to live is Christ and to die is gain* (Philippians 1:21) and *I count everything as loss because of the surpassing worth of knowing Christ Jesus my Lord. For His sake I have suffered the loss of all things, and count them as refuse, in order that I may gain Christ . . .* (Philippians 3:8).

Paul's pulsating motivation was both to know Christ and to make Him better known. He was an evangelist. His life's work and calling was to proclaim the Good News of the crucified Christ, explaining *it pleased God through the folly of what we preach to save those who believe* (1 Corinthians 1:21). Christ crucified may seem foolish to the non-Christian, yet every true Christian knows that *the word of the cross is folly to those who are perish-*

ing, but to us who are being saved it is the power of God . . . For the foolishness of God is wiser than men (1 Corinthians 1:18,25). Paul then, inspite of his high background, was glad to think of himself as Christ's fool.

The three fools: the atheist, materialist and evangelist. The question is 'Whose fool am I?'

In closing, consider the words of a 20th century Christian martyr, Jim Elliot. He lost (or should we say gained) his life in the service of Christ overseas. Before he died he said this: "He is no fool who gives what he cannot keep to gain what he cannot lose."

Chapter Nineteen

THE HAIR OF
THE BIBLE

❖

Hair and hair styles often become a subject of contention
between parents and children. When one wants one style,
the other wants the opposite, and an argument begins.
The 'in' style for many young people is usually the same style as
their favourite pop star, footballer or other role model – irrespective of whether such actually suits their face.

    The Bible has something to say about our hair on top, as
we shall now see:-

    1. In 1 Corinthians 11:14,15 we read *Does not nature itself
teach you that for a man to wear long hair is degrading for him,
but if a woman has long hair it is her pride?* The Bible, you see,
emphasises that male and female is the divine order, and anything which blurs or denies this distinction (e.g. homosexuality,
transexuality or unisexuality) is against both nature and the will

of God. *Male and female He created them* reads Genesis 1:27.
This being so, we can understand the stern warning of Deuteronomy 22:5 that *A woman shall not wear anything that pertains
to a man, nor shall a man put on a woman's garment; for
whoever does these things is an abomination to the Lord your
God.*

2. Matthew 10:30 reassures us *even the hairs of your head
are all numbered.* Whilst you would be hard pressed to say just
how many hairs are on the head of your spouse or closest friend,
this verse assures us that God's knowledge of us is so intimate
that He even knows the number of the hairs on our head. God
knows us better than we know ourselves. He is well acquainted
with all of our hopes, fears, troubles, cares, difficulties and
frustrations. Our physical condition is well known to Him. Our
psychological and emotional make-up is well known to Him too.
(For what it is worth, a barber once explained that the average
head has an estimated 360,000 hairs - less on a ginger head, and
more on a blonde head).

3. In Revelation 1:14,15 John catches a glimpse of the
glorified Christ. He describes Him thus: *His head and His hair
were white as white wool, white as snow, His eyes were like a
flame of fire . . .* Awesome. It reminds us that Jesus is Lord. Yes,
He is a Saviour to trust. Yes, He is a friend to love, but also, He is
God, and as God He is to be worshipped and adored. When John
saw this particular hair on this particular Person's head he tells us
When I saw Him, I fell at His feet as though dead (Revelation
1:17). We see here that Christianity is not so much a topic of
discussion or a philosophy to consider, but rather, Christianity
concerns a Person to be worshipped. Interestingly, the Greek word
for worship is 'proskuneo,' which means 'to fall down/to pros-
trate oneself before.'

4. In Luke 7 we read about a rather disreputable woman
who came up to Jesus and weep*ing, she began to wet His feet
with her tears, and wiped them with the hair of her head.* She

was devoted to Jesus with no inhibitions whatsoever. Why? Well Jesus said that it was because she had experienced His forgiveness of all her sins. Jesus explained *Therefore I tell you, her sins, which are many, are forgiven, for she loved much; but he who is forgiven little loves little* (Luke 7:47). And it is still the same today. Those who are unaware of their sin will never see their need of Jesus. But those who are aware of their sins, and come to Jesus for forgiveness - a forgiveness available because of the blood which He shed on the cross (Hebrews 9:22) - can only love Him and want to worship Him. Forgiveness is fuel for our worship. Forgiveness - God's forgiveness - is the source of the soul's eternal well being. It is the blessing of all who know Jesus as their own personal Saviour. The blessing only comes through faith in Jesus, but can be experienced by those with dark hair, grey hair, fair hair or even no hair at all.

My sin, O the bliss of this glorious thought
My sin, not the part but the whole
Is nailed to the cross, and I bear it no more
Praise the Lord, praise the Lord, O my soul.

Chapter Twenty

THE PRECIOUS THINGS
OF THE BIBLE

❖

The BBC programme The Antiques Roadshow has a large following. In this programme we see people bringing their family treasures and heirlooms to be valued by the experts in such matters. The precious and sentimental items are usually worth very little, but now and again a person has a very pleasant surprise, and realises that they are a lot richer than they thought they were.

Turning from porcelain to people, how much do you think that you are worth? The answer of course depends on what and who you think you are. Here is some interesting data. Did you know that, on a purely material or physical level, the average person weighing 70 kg has, distributed in their body:-

enough carbon to make 9,000 pencils
enough phosphorus to make 2,200 match heads
enough fat to make 7 bars of soap
enough water to fill a 45 litre (10 gallon) barrel and
enough iron to make one 2" nail.

So we are worth something then – but not much!

All this goes to show that price is not to be confused with value. Whilst something may not be worth very much in monetary terms, it can still be extremely valuable and precious. In this chapter I should like us to consider some of the literally 'precious things' of the Bible:-

1. Precious Love

In Psalm 36:7, the Psalmist exclaims: *How precious is Thy steadfast love, O God!* The precious, steadfast love of God? Surely this is the most precious commodity of all. God's 'steadfast love' has been variously translated as His covenant love; His faithfulness; His committed love; His loving kindness; His constant, unfluctuating, grace and mercy to His people. How precious this love is. It is both the origination and continuation of every blessing we have and every blessing we will ever have. How totally and infinitely unlike the love of this world is the love of God. We will have cause to recourse to God's precious, steadfast love every day of our earthly pilgrimage. *Keep yourselves in the love of God* (Jude 21).

2. Precious Blood

You know that you were ransomed . . . with the precious blood of Christ (1 Peter 1:18,19) wrote Peter. The precious blood of Christ. Its value must be infinite because it was able to purchase such a great multitude of souls – no less than God's

Church throughout the ages. *The church of God which He obtained with the blood of His own Son* (Acts 20:28). Christ's blood owes its preciousness and efficacy from the fact that it is the blood of none less that the Son of God, the Word made flesh – hence its potency, power and price. How precious is the blood of Christ to the believer. Through His blood shed at Calvary we have innumerable blessings:- pardon, peace, justification, reconciliation, redemption . . . no wonder the song of heaven is a song which continues Peter's 'precious' theme: *Thou was slain and by Thy blood didst ransom men for God* (Revelation 5:9).

> Oh wondrous is the crimson tide
> Which from my Saviour flowed!
> And still in heaven my song shall be
> "The precious, precious blood!"

3. Precious Promises

In 2 Peter 1:4 we read that God *has granted to us His precious and very great promises.* How do we know we are saved? Because God has promised us salvation in His Word. No wonder then that these promises are precious to us. God's Word promises eternal life to all who believe in Jesus. In the Bible we have the *hope of eternal life which God, who never lies, promised ages ago* (Titus 1:2).

4. Precious Faith

. . . *like precious faith* . . . (2 Peter 1:1 KJV). Faith too is precious. The bond of a common Faith between believers is better experienced than described. The Christian Faith has a corporate as well as an individual aspect to it. Salvation brings us into fellowship with the people of God as well as with God Himself. The bond of Faith destroys the man-made barriers of race, class, nationality, colour, age and occupation. How we should value our *like precious faith* and do all we can to further the harmony of God's church.

> Blest be the tie that binds
> Our hearts in Christian love
> The fellowship of kindred minds
> Is like to that above.

5. Precious Death

Precious in the sight of the Lord is the death of His saints (Psalm 116:15). It must be so. God's saints, that is His 'set apart ones' have been chosen by Him for glory in eternity past. Then in time, God sent His Son to die to save these chosen people. Still in time, God sent His Spirit to regenerate these people for whom Christ died. One day, in God's own time, God will call each individual chosen in Christ to be with Himself, *away from the body and at home with the Lord* (2 Corinthians 5:8).

Being called into God's nearer presence will be a most precious experience. For us - a precious experience which will never be surpassed. Amazingly though, the Bible reveals that it is an experience precious to Almighty God too, for *Precious in the sight of the Lord is the death of His saints.*

In a valueless world then, here are some precious things of the Bible: our God's love is precious to us; our Saviour's blood is precious to us; the promises of God are precious to us; our common Faith is precious to us, and the day of our death, a date already written in God's diary, is especially precious to Him.

Chapter Twenty-One

THE NOTHINGS OF
THE BIBLE

❖

A famous Bishop of the established church had been invited to preach in a small country church. Afterwards, one elderly parishoner was met outside by her son, who asked her, "Well, how was it? What did the Bishop have to say?" In reply, his mother gave a little shrug of her shoulders and said, "Oh. Nothing much at all really."

How anyone can speak for twenty minutes or so and say absolutely nothing is a mystery. Perhaps the good Bishop spoke above the lady's head. Or perhaps her mind was so distracted by other things that she failed to give him her full attention. Someone has said, 'One man's meat is another man's poison.' Similarly, a sermon which has one person on the end of her seat may have another at the end of her tether!

This chapter is going to be about nothing. If that statement does not make any sense to you, read on and understand some of the important 'nothings' of the Bible:-

1. 1 Timothy 6:6,7 reads *There is great gain in godliness with contentment, for we brought <u>nothing</u> into the world, and we cannot take anything out of the world.* There is our first 'nothing'. *We brought nothing into the world, and we cannot take anything out of the world* says Paul. He possibly had Job 1:21 in mind when he wrote: *Naked I came from my mother's womb and naked I shall return* or possibly Psalm 49:17 which says of the rich man *when he dies he will carry nothing away; his glory will not go down after him.*

It is a sobering thought that actually we do not own anything. Yet from the Bible's perspective, it helps us to get our priorities right and seek the true and lasting riches from God's right hand. Jesus had the true riches in mind when He exhorted: *Do not lay up for yourselves treasures on earth, where moth and rust consume and where thieves break in and steal, but lay up for yourselves treasures in heaven, where neither moth nor rust consumes and where thieves do not break in and steal* (Matthew 6:19,20).

2. A second 'nothing' is also contained in some words of Jesus to His disciples. Jesus said *I am the vine. You are the branches. He who abides in Me and I in him, he it is that bears much fruit, for apart from Me you can do <u>nothing</u>* (John 15:5). Jesus is talking here about the necessity of a close union with Himself if we are to avoid a wasted, fruitless life. Just as a branch abides in the main vine, draws on its sap and produces fruit, so likewise the Christian is to abide in Jesus and know His 'life giving sap' flowing into the soul. There is no salvation apart from personal faith in Jesus. Acts 4:12 is crystal clear: *And there is salvation in no one else for there is no other name under heaven given among men by which we must be saved.* But John 15:5 tells us that us that we are to continue abiding in Jesus if our lives

are to bear spiritual fruit. *Apart from Me you can do nothing* states Jesus. A self-sufficient, self-reliant Christian is no more true than a square circle or hot ice. Christianity is a vital, living, on-going relationship with Jesus *the true vine.*

3. In one of the most famous and lyrical passages of the Bible, Paul reminds us that without the gift and grace of love, we are nothing. The well loved passage in 1 Corinthians 13 explains:- *If I speak in the tongues of men and of angels, but have not love, I am a noisy gong or a clanging cymbal. And if I have prophetic powers, and understand all mysteries and all knowledge, and if I have faith, so as to remove mountains, but have not love, I am nothing. If I give away all I have, and if I deliver my body to be burned, but have not love, I gain nothing . . .*

If I am lacking in love then, I am nothing, says the Bible, and that is most unsettling. Paraphrasing Paul, "If I could understand the Bible and gain a Doctorate of Divinity. If I could pack out a church and be a nationally famous preacher. If I could publish best selling books on the Christian Faith . . . but if I have not the love of God flowing out to others I am nothing, for my activities would be all empty, external works of the flesh. " Love then is the distinguishing mark of a Christian. *God's love has been poured into our hearts through the Holy Spirit which has been given to us* (Romans 5:5). *He who does not love does not know God, for God is love* (1 John 4:8). *A new commandment I give to you, that you love one another; even as I have loved you, that you also love one another* (John 13:14). That should drive us to knees, asking God to forgive our unloving attitudes and ways and asking Him to help us fulfil His commandment to love as He is love, and in His love sent His beloved Son to be our Saviour.

This chapter is almost finished and it has been filled it up with nothings! To re-cap:-

1. We have nothing and are nothing apart from our relationship with God.

2. Jesus said *apart from Me you can do nothing.*

3. Paul stated that *if I have not love, I am nothing.*

So may God, by His Holy Spirit, shed more of the love and life and light of Jesus into all of our hearts, and so make somethings out of nothings.

Chapter Twenty-Two

THE DOORS OF
THE BIBLE

❖

One of the most traumatic 'rites of passage' in life is our first move away from the security of our family and home, forcing us to take sole responsibility for our personal finance, clothes, food and household security. The move from a communal to an individual existence takes quite a lot of readjustment. Buck passing is now not an option! Often, too, when we have left our new residence for any reason, halfway through the morning a panic sets in "Did I turn the gas off?" "Did I close all the windows?" and even "I can't remember closing my front door." It is odd how we can never seem to recall actions which we do automatically – such as locking our front door behind us.

Doors. We do not think about them much, and yet they are vital. They let the relevant people in and they keep the unwanted, undesirable people out. I notice that the Bible has a few doors which we can open too:-

1. In John 10:7 Jesus says *I am the door of the sheep.* And in John 10:9 He says *I am the door; if any one enters by Me, he will be saved, and will go in and out and find pasture.* In Bible times, sheepfolds had no actual doors, but just a space through which the sheep could enter and exit. This being so, the shepherd himself would lie across the entrance to the sheepfold at night, effectively becoming its 'door.' Sheep could thus only enter through him, and he also was the one who kept them safe once inside – fending off the wolves and other undesirables out to harm and damage the flock. From this we can see that it is through Jesus that we enter into eternal life and salvation: *I am the door; if anyone enters by Me he will be saved.* We also see from this that it is through Jesus that we are kept eternally safe. He was to say a little later *I give them (My sheep) eternal life, and they shall never perish, and no one shall snatch them out of My hand* (John 10:28).

2. Interestingly, the first mention of a door in the Bible occurs in Genesis 6:16, when God commanded Noah to make an ark. The Divine instructions included . . . *set the door of the ark in its side* (Genesis 6:16). The wickedness of the world was so great in those days, that God saw fit to judge it by a great, universal flood. There was salvation for Noah and his family in the ark however. The waters of judgement just could not harm them at all, for they were safe behind the ark's door. Genesis 7:16 tells us that *the Lord shut him in.* So what a 'type' of the Lord Jesus Christ is the ark! He is the One Who saves all who trust in Him from eternal judgement. *Jesus . . . delivers us from the wrath to come* (1 Thessalonians 1:10).

3. There is a further reference to doors in the time of Moses, when the tabernacle, or 'tent of meeting' was built. God Himself, although everywhere, condescended to presence Himself in this special tent in a very special way. Every detail of

the tabernacle speaks of Christ – the Word Who was to become flesh and tabernacle Himself among us (cf John 1:14).

The tabernacle only had one door however, and the first item of furniture to be met on entering was the large altar of burnt offering. Exodus 40:6:- *You shall set the altar of burnt offering before the door of the tabernacle of the tent of meeting.* What a picture! There is only one way to God and that is through Jesus. He said *I am the way and the truth and the life, no one comes to the Father but by Me* (John 14:6). And the only way to God is through the 'altar' of Calvary where Jesus was sacrificed, shedding His blood for the forgiviness of sins and the reconciliation of sinners to God.

4. In Colossians 4:3, the Apostle Paul makes the following request: *Pray for us also, that God may open to us a door for the Word.* And in Acts 14:27 we read of a report given at a church gathering which *declared all that God had done with them, and how He had opened up a door of faith to the Gentiles.* It is a very humbling truth to realise that only God can open the door of our hearts and shine his light into them. If we are Christians in this predominantly non-Christian world therefore, how grateful we have cause to be. God Himself by His Spirit has opened up our hearts and minds to our sin and need – and God Himself, by His Spirit has enabled us to appropriate His provision for our sin and need in the Saviour. This apart, what about obeying Paul's request and asking that God in His grace will open the hearts of some of our non-Christian friends to Jesus?

5. Finally, in Revelation 4:1,2, we have the most remarkable vision. John records *After this I looked, and lo, in heaven an open door!* Here then we are given nothing less than a glimpse of the glory! But what did John see? He saw *a throne stood in heaven, with One seated on the throne.* How good and comforting it is to know that, even in these days, when things can

seem so difficult, dark, dangerous and discouraging, and evil, at
times, seems to be winning, that our God is still the *God Who is
seated on the throne. . . . Hallelujah! For the Lord our God the
Almighty reigns* (Revelation 19:4,6).

So there are some of the doors of Scripture. We will end
with one of the gracious invitations of the risen and reigning Lord
Jesus when He said *Behold, I stand at the door and knock.; if any
one hears My voice and opens the door, I will come in to him and
eat with him, and he with Me* (Revelation 3:20).

There's a way back to God, from the dark paths of sin
There's a door that is open and you may go in
At Calvary's cross is where you begin
When you come as a sinner to Jesus

Chapter Twenty-Three

THE SOLACE OF
THE BIBLE

❖

Not one of us lives in a germ-free bubble, removed from the hard and harsh realities of this fallen world. At some stage in our lives we will all have to cope with some kind of tragedy which strikes seemingly without any mercy at all, leaving us totally paralysed, pulverised and perplexed. Sudden bereavement, for example, can change our whole outlook on life in a moment – as does a sudden redundancy or the experience of a life-threatening illness to either ourselves or someone we love. The big question is, how can we cope when life appears to go so desperately, hopelessly, cruelly and callously wrong? I offer the following thoughts from the Bible:–

1. Realise that no matter how dire our circumstances may seem, God is on the throne. Realise that there are no accidents with

Him as He has foreordained absolutely everything which comes
to pass. He is too wise to make mistakes, and too loving to be
unkind. I read in the Bible of God that *from Him and through
Him and to Him are all things* (Romans 11:36). The Bible assures us that God is in control of absolutely every major and mi-
nor event of our lives for *The LORD has established His throne
in the heavens, and His kingdom rules over all* (Psalm 103: 19),
and Jesus said *Are not two sparrows sold for a penny? And not
one of them will fall to the ground without YOUR FATHER'S
WILL* (Matthew 10:29). All this is most reassuring. God knows
all about our disasters and devastations. They do not take Him by
surprise or 'off guard', for it is He who actually is the ultimate
cause of them. Oh to be able to take the harsher providences in
the same manner as the kinder ones – and even to kiss the hand
that chastises us.

2. In Psalm 46:1 we read:– *God is our refuge and strength, a very
present help in trouble,* and verse 7 of the same Psalm reads *The
Lord of hosts is with us; the God of Jacob is our refuge.* That title
the God of Jacob is most instructive. Jacob was such a devious
trickster and 'wheeler and dealer'. The title *the God of Jacob*
speaks volumes about God's grace, that is, His love and favour
to the undeserving and ill-deserving.

The Bible, then, assures us of God's help in and through
our suffering. Maybe, in His wisdom, that is why God sends us
trouble and sorrow – would we seek Him so earnestly otherwise?
Seek the Lord and His strength, seek His presence continually
(Psalm 105:4).

The Apostle Paul reported to the church at Corinth that at
one time, he was in such pain through a *thorn in the flesh,* that
Three times I besought the Lord about this that it should leave me
(2 Corinthians 12:8). If anyone was a man of God Paul was – yet
God did not answer his prayers for deliverance. Instead, God gave
him grace to cope. God said to him *My grace is sufficient for you,*

for my power is made perfect in weakness. What a promise for you and me to claim! *MY GRACE IS SUFFICIENT FOR YOU!* It is so easy to complain. Perish the thought that we should ever rail against God instead of seeking help from God. To whom else can we go? Where else can we even fall? The Bible says *The eternal God is your dwelling place, and underneath are the everlasting arms* (Deuteronomy 33:27).

3. Troubles, trials and tragedies make us realise just how weak we are, and just how fragile is the world in which we live. In the 'School of Adversity' we are taught that our relationship with God is our only certainty in life and death. Health fails. Friends may fail. Loved ones may die. Poverty may hit us. Redundancy may strike with no mercy . . . but the Bible assures us *I the Lord do not change* (Malachi 3:6).

In Psalm 73, the Psalmist, at first, did what many of us do: he murmured about the perceived injustices of this life, when the ungodly do well and prosper, whilst God's people seem to suffer. But then he came to his senses and thought 'theo-logically' rather than logically, and confessed to God:– *Whom have I in heaven but Thee? And there is nothing upon earth that I desire besides Thee. My flesh and my heart may fail, but GOD is the strength of my heart and my portion for ever* (Psalm 73:25,26).

He knew God as his 'portion' – and so may we if we belong to Jesus. And it makes all the difference in the world.

> Rest in the Lord, O weary, heavy-laden
> Look unto Him, your ever-present Guide
> Rest in the Lord, whose Word is truth eternal
> Leave all to Him, whatever may betide
>
> Rest in the Lord, and tell Him all your sorrow
> Trust in His love, so boundless, full and free
> He will not leave, nor will He e'er forsake you
> Rest in the Lord, and sweet your rest shall be.

Chapter Twenty-Four

THE GENTLEMAN OF
THE BIBLE

❖

W hatever the rights and wrongs of fox hunting are - and
it is a 'blood sport' which has beome increasingly
controversial in recent years - if you have ever
attended a hunt, you will no doubt have been impressed by the
sight and spectacle, with its well groomed horses ridden by
gentlemen in their finery, along with the distinctive sound of hunting horns. I used the word 'gentlemen' because a huntsman seems
to be a perfect depiction which illustrates the term 'the perfect
gentleman'.

Did you know that the Jesus described in the Bible is the
only truly 'perfect gentleman' that has ever lived? Here, however, I am not referring to gentleman in the sense of a chivalrous,
well bred huntsman, but rather to that quality of Christ's life
characterised by tenderness and mildness and His not being too

rough or severe to those who came to Him in need. Jesus truly is the perfect gentle-man.

Christ's gentleness is not the whole story mind you. He always called a spade a spade and did not shrink from condemning hypocrisy and injustice – not to mention giving severe warnings about the reality of eternal punishment. Jesus warned about hell to unbelievers as much as He promised heaven to believers. But in this chapter, let us consider the gentleness of Christ. It certainly has much to encourage us with as we go through the rough and tumble of daily living:-

It was written prophetically of Jesus: *a bruised reed He will not break, and a dimly burning wick He will not quench* (Isaiah 42:3). Sometimes circumstances make us feel like that bruised reed. Events happen that make us feel that there is no light at the end of the tunnel we find ourselves in. Be assured that Jesus knows. Be assured that Jesus cares. He alone can bind up our bruises. He alone can ensure that our feeble light will not be extinguished. Jesus, the master carpenter, is an expert in putting back together the broken pieces of our fragile lives – and how tenderly He does it.

Consider next Jesus' life on earth. Where do we begin? Well what about His gentle dealings with lepers? In biblical times leprosy had a social stigma on a par with present day AIDS. But in Jesus' ministry lepers were cleansed – cleansed instantly by His tender touch – when no one in his right mind would have gone near such defiled outcasts. Then there was that woman caught in adultery. The Scribes and Pharisees were all for strict justice, and keen on stoning her, adding the death penalty to her sin and shame. But they all slunk away when Jesus said *Let him who is without sin among you be the first to throw a stone at her* and when they had all gone, Jesus said to the woman *Neither do I condemn you; go and sin no more* (See John 8 1-11).

Time and space would fail us to mention the many practical examples of Jesus' compassion, be it to an individual widow, struck by tragedy and grief; two equally bereaved parents of a little girl, or even to five thousand plus people who were hungry. Jesus disturbed the comfortable, yes. He upset the complacent status quo at times. But He also comforted the disturbed too. Remember His gracious and tender invitation: *Come to me all who labour and are heavy laden and I will give you rest. Take my yoke upon you and learn from me, for I am gentle and lowly in heart and you will find rest for your souls* . . . (Matthew 11:28 ff.).

You may well say though something like "But that was then, and this is now. Can Jesus really help me in my present plight and predicament?" The wonderful news is that He can! Jesus has lost none of His understanding, compassion, tenderness, gentleness and power, for we read in the Bible that *Jesus Christ is the same yesterday and today and for ever* (Hebrews 13: 8).

Jesus' main speciality is in saving sinners. When aware of the burden of our sin, and plagued by a guilty conscience, we may be assured that Jesus will never turn us away (John 6:37). He is the friend of sinners. He died for sinners. He shed His blood so that our sins can be forgiven. 'Come every soul with guilt oppressed there's mercy with the Lord!'

When going through some intolerable trial, every Christian has the privilege of being able to take it to the Lord in prayer. The Bible has the encouragement that *we have not a high priest who is unable to sympathise with our weaknesses, but one who in every respect has been tempted as we are, yet without sin. Let us then with confidence draw near to the throne of grace, that we may receive mercy and find grace to help in time of need* (Hebrews 4:15,16).

Lastly though, what if we feel that we have failed God? Such is a dreadful feeling. Christians who once walked on the straight and narrow seem to have further to fall, but Jesus understands even this. His arms are wide open for us. There is restoration with Him, just as He restored Peter after he had let Jesus down so badly (see John 21). So whatever is weighing our conscience down, we may take heart from the following promise of the Bible when it tells us that *if we confess our sins He is faithful and just and will forgive our sins and cleanse us from all unrighteousness* (1 John 1:9).

So what a tender Friend we have in Jesus. He is the Friend we need in this fallen world, with its headaches, heartaches and heartbreaks. Be reassured that Jesus will deal most compassionately, tenderly and gently with whatever need you may have. Spread your need before Him, for He is the perfect gentle-man.

God will take care of you – be not afraid
He is your safeguard, thru' sunshine and shade
Tenderly watching and keeping His own
He will not leave you to wander alone

God will take care of you still to the end
Oh what a Father, redeemer and friend
Jesus will answer wherever you call
He will take care of you, trust Him for all.

Chapter Twenty-Five

THE RELIGION OF
THE BIBLE

❖

'The Bible and the Bible alone is the religion of Protestants' – so wrote William Chillingworth in the last century. It is a happy dictum. Protestantism is a religion of the Book – the Book of God and God of all books, the Bible.

On the British mainland, we do not hear the word 'Protestant' used very often to describe a Christian. It is very different in Northern Ireland though. Those of us who have lived in Northern Ireland know that it is characterised by a religious divide, and 'sitting on the fence' is not an option. An apocryphal tale tells how a Jew once visited Belfast and was immediately asked: "What are you, a Protestant or a Catholic." When he replied "I'm actually Jewish" the immediate retort was "But are you a Catholic or a Protestant Jew."

The word 'Protestant' has negative connotations in some people's minds, as they associate it solely with negative 'protests' against religious error. In actual fact though, the word 'Protestant' is a positive one, for it means 'a witness to the truth' – the truth of God as revealed in the Bible.

A Catholic in Belfast once said that the Protestant Faith was relatively recent "going back to Henry VIII and his wives." Protestantism actually goes back much further than that though, for Protestantism goes back to the Bible. Protestantism, that is Biblical Christianity, can be summarised by saying 'The Bible alone, which teaches that we are saved by God's grace alone, through faith alone in Jesus Christ alone, to the glory of God alone.'

For this chapter then, let us consider four 'open things' of the Protestant Faith. These are:- 1. An Open Bible 2. An Open Fountain 3. An Open Throne and 4. An Open Heaven.

1. An Open Bible

For Protestants, the Bible alone is the sole source of authority for belief and practice. The Bible is nothing less than God's Word written, and thus the authority of the Bible is nothing less than the authority of God Himself. It is the Bible that bears witness to Jesus Christ and His death on the cross to save sinners. *Christ died for our sins in accordance with the Scriptures* (1 Corinthians 15:3). All the roads of the Bible lead to Calvary. It is anticipated in the Old Testament, described in the Gospels, preached in the Acts, explained and applied in the epistles and generally celebrated throughout.

An open Bible is the glory of Protestantism. God wrote the Bible through His Holy Spirit's working through the human authors (cf 2 Timothy 3:16 and 2 Peter 1:21). His divine superintendence thus ensures it is wholly free from error. Furthermore, not only did God write the Bible by His Holy Spirit, but He promises to give us the help of the Holy Spirit to enable us to understand the Book which He wrote. God promises the help of the Holy Spirit to all who will ask for such help in humility. We will never be able to understand the Bible and God's gracious promise of salvation written therein without the Holy Spirit's aid. Paul wrote: *we have received . . . the Spirit which is from God, that we might understand the gifts bestowed by God* (1 Corinthians 2:12), but also, by way of negation *The natural man does not receive the gifts of the Spirit of God, for they are folly to him, and he is not able to understand them because they are spiritually discerned* (1 Corinthians 2:14). The open Bible for all then, is one of the glories of Protestantism.

2. An Open Fountain

In the Old Testament, God made this promise: *There shall be a fountain opened for the house of David and the inhabitants of Jerusalem to cleanse them from sin and unclean-ness* (Zechariah 13:1). This cleansing fountain - so imperative if we are ever going to approach a holy God - refers to none other than Jesus Christ. The Bible is crystal clear. *The blood of Jesus His Son cleanses us from all sin* (1 John 1:7). This is the glory of Protestantism. Peter refers to *the precious blood of Christ* (1 Peter 1:18), and the subject is the theme of literally thousands of hymns:-

> There is a fountain filled with blood
> drawn from Emmanuel's veins
> Sinners who plunge beneath that flood
> lose all their guilty stains.

3. An Open Throne

Protestantism affirms a direct access to God Himself. Think of that! Through Christ we are able to have an audience with the King of kings! The Bible knows nothing of going to God through a human priest, pope, 'saint' or statue. The Bible teaches that we have direct access to God through Jesus Christ. *Let us then with confidence draw near to the throne of grace, that we may receive mercy and find grace to help in time of need* (Hebrews 4:16). It is to the God of the Bible that we can go with all our needs – including our need of daily forgiveness. We confess our sins to Him and He pardons them on the basis of Christ's death. *If we confess our sins He is faithful and just and will forgive our sins and cleanse us from all unrighteousness* (1 John 1:9).

Finally though, the true glory of Protestantism is actually yet to be. Protestantism proclaims not just an open Bible, fountain and throne, but also:-

4. An Open Heaven

'Truly, I say to you, today you will be with Me in Paradise' (Luke 23:43) promised the Lord Jesus to a dying thief. The dying thief was thus a Protestant! He was a sinner saved by grace. He went from the gallows to the glory, from pain to Paradise because of the mercy of God in Jesus Christ.

We too can be sure of a home in heaven if we are trusting Jesus. His blood really does cleanse us from sin and fit us for heaven. *In Paradise* promised Jesus. The Bible speaks of only two eternal destinations, heaven or hell. Its sixty six books contain no mention of any supposed 'Purgatory' at all. Heaven is gained and hell is shunned only by personal faith in Christ crucified. Protestantism is the religion of the Bible and gladly proclaims a divine salvation, freely given in Jesus Christ. Salvation according to the Bible is by grace alone, through faith alone in the crucified Christ alone, for

> There was no other good enough
> To pay the price of sin
> He only could unlock the gate
> Of heaven and let us in.

Chapter Twenty-Six

THE CHEERS OF
THE BIBLE

❖

A word in season, how good it is! (Proverbs 15:23), to which
we can all reply with a hearty 'Amen!' for *Pleasant words
are like a honeycomb, sweetness to the soul and health to
the body* Proverbs 16:24).

There are some days when we need a word of cheer more
than others – Monday mornings, for instance, or returning to work
or school after the holidays, or when we find ourselves lying on a
hospital bed. Being human, we all have our 'off days' and 'down-
ers'. How we deal with these, I suggest, is one measure of our
maturity as a Christian. Trials and difficulties, disappointments
and set backs can reveal our true character far more than when
things are all smooth, swinging, happy and plain sailing.

In this chapter, I should like us to consider not three,
but four 'cheers' from the Bible. These cheers are ours to enjoy

irrespective of our circumstances. These 'cheers' all come from the lips of Jesus and have been variously translated as *Take heart* or *Be of good cheer.* You will see that they really are just what the doctor ordered! All the cheers were spoken to anxious souls, illustrating the truth of Proverbs 12:25:*Anxiety in a man's heart weighs him down, but a good word makes him glad.*

1. The Cheer of His Pardon

In Matthew 9:2 we read Jesus saying *Take heart, my son, your sins are forgiven.* These were certainly cheerful words to the one addressed, as he was a paralysed man. But no sooner had Jesus given him this word of pardon than he rose up, folded up the mat on which he was carried and went joyfully on his way.

We can do the same if we have heard Jesus' word of pardon to our souls. Divine forgiveness is so liberating. Divine forgiveness is possible because Jesus died for our sins on the cross, shedding His blood for our forgiveness. If we have experienced the pardoning power of the blood of Jesus, we know that ultimately all is well with our souls. Hear Jesus' cheerful words again: *Take heart, my son, your sins are forgiven. . . . Who can forgive sins but God alone?* (Mark 2:7). Good question! Jesus is God.

2. The Cheer of His Peace

Take heart, it is I, have no fear (Matthew 14:27) said Jesus on another occasion. They were such welcome words, uttered amidst the most terrible and fearful storm out at sea in the middle of the night. The storm threatened to engulf those frightened disciples in their little, powerless boat.

We all know the feeling. The storms of life can make us feel so weak, vulnerable and helpless when we are tossed about in our feeble 'little boats.' How welcome Jesus's words are therefore to us: *Take heart, it is I, have no fear.* Jesus stands by us in and through the storms of life. Jesus can calm the stormiest of waters that we go through or will ever go through, as He is Lord of heaven and earth. *Have no fear* , He says.

I am told that there are three hundred and sixty six 'Fear nots' in the Bible. If that is true, there is one for every day of the year, including a leap year for good measure. The cheer of His peace. *Thou dost keep him in perfect peace, whose mind is stayed on Thee, because he trusts in Thee. Trust in the Lord for ever, for the Lord God is an everlasting rock* (Isaiah 26:3,4).

3. The Cheer of His Power

In John 16:33 Jesus says *In the world you have tribulation; but be of good cheer. I have overcome the world.* In this world we all certainly have had, or will have tribulation. How good then to know that Jesus is greater than all our tribulations. By His death and resurrection Jesus overcame the world and all its evil. He is its ruler. God is in charge! There is a lovely chorus:-

> This is my Father's world
> and may I ne'er forget
> that though the wrong
> seems e'er so strong
> God is the ruler yet

God is on the throne and He will not and cannot be over-thrown. Therefore, whatever we are going through or will have to go through before we reach glory, all is ultimately well.

4. The Cheer of His Presence

In the closing chapters of Acts we read of the apostle Paul's journeying to the unknown, no doubt fearful for his life as he had every reason to be. His future was most uncertain, and all things being equal, all he had to look forward to was pain and discomfort. But at this very time we read this: *The following night the Lord stood by him and said 'Take courage'* (Acts 23:11). And if we are Christ's, no matter how fearful the conditions, He will stand by us too. The cheer of His presence. He promises us *I will never fail you nor forsake you* (Hebrews 13:5) – and His promises are true and dependable. What a friend we have in Jesus! He is the *Friend Who sticks closer than a brother (Proverbs 18:24)*.He is a Friend for life, death, and praise His name, for all eternity.

So here then are four cheers for cheerless days – timely cheers for us all. The cheer of His pardon, His peace, His power and His blessed presence in our lives now and for ever.

Who can cheer the heart like Jesus, by His presence all Divine?
True and tender, pure and precious, O how blest to call Him mine!

All that thrills my soul is Jesus; He is more than life to me
And the fairest of ten thousand, in my blessed Lord I see.

Chapter Twenty-Seven

THE SWEAT OF
THE BIBLE

❖

Those of us who enjoy long distance running for a hobby sometimes covet having a 'Goretex' suit in which to run on rainy days. Running in the rain wearing an ordinary anorak has its drawbacks – we seem to get wetter on the inside from perspiration and condensation than we do from the rain outside. An expensive 'Goretex' suit however would solve the problem, for 'Goretex' fibre is breathable – it has a special constitution which lets perspiration out but does not let rain water in.

My subject now is the unusual one of sweat. Not the politest of subjects you might say. Boys are taught that horses sweat, men perspire and ladies just 'get a little hot.'

The word 'sweat' occurs only three times in the whole Bible. Three times only, but three very significant times, as we shall now see:-

1. The first occurrence of the word 'sweat' is in Genesis 3:19, way back in the garden of Eden. After our first ancestors had sinned, God made the pronouncement: *In the sweat of your face you shall eat bread till you return to the ground, for out of it you were taken; you are dust and to dust you shall return.* Sweat then, is part of the curse of sin – just as much as the thorns, thistles and heavy labour which all resulted from a world out of harmony with its Maker. When sin came in, God cursed the ground. Formerly most fruitful, it now required effort to be cultivated, and so beads of sweat appeared on Adam's brow for the first time.

2. The second occurrence of the word 'sweat' in the Bible is in Ezekiel 44:18. There, God's instructions to the Levitical priests included this: *They shall have linen turbans upon their heads, and linen breeches upon their loins; they shall not gird themselves with anything that causes sweat.*

The priests in Old Testament times ministered in the sanctuary of God Himself. Both the service and the place was holy, as everything to do with God is. This being so, sin, the antithesis of holiness, had no place there. The priests were thus commanded not to wear anything that would cause sweat. Their very garments were made and worn with this in mind.

What a picture all this is of the Lord Jesus Christ. Christ is *our great high priest* (Hebrews 4:14). Whereas the Old Testament priests' garments alluded to purity, Christ was sinless perfection, spotless purity and immaculate holiness itself. The Old Testament priesthood foreshadowed and prefigured the Lord Jesus Christ. Christ, the sinless One, would eventually come and fulfil the Old Testament priesthood and sacrificial system when He bore our sins in His body on the tree of Calvary's sacrifice.

Ezekiel's mention of the word 'sweat' was about one thousand years after Moses had written the same word in the book of Genesis. But in Luke's Gospel, written some five hundred years after Ezekiel, we have the third and final use of the word 'sweat' in the Bible:-

3. Luke 22:44 records this of Jesus in Gethsemane's garden: *being in agony He prayed earnestly; and His sweat became like great drops of blood falling down upon the ground.* Here, in contemplating the cross, Jesus contemplated the imminent and indescribable sufferings He was about to undergo on the sinner's behalf. It made Him sweat. On the cross, the Bible says, Jesus, the sinless One, was actually made to bear our sins and God's wrath and judgement upon them, so we might be saved. Sin caused and causes sweat. Jesus was to bear our sins, so no wonder the thought made Him sweat. The sweat was so intense that it fell as great drops of blood, falling down upon the ground which God had cursed all those millennia before. The Bible assures all who belong to Jesus *Christ redeemed us from the curse of the law having become a curse for us, for it is written 'cursed be every one who hangs on a tree'* (Galatians 3:13).

So there are the three occurrences of the word 'sweat' in the Bible. The three writers could never collude as centuries separated them, but they certainly did not collide either. It is one of the many undesigned evidences that the Bible is nothing less than the Word of God, written down for us. Its remarkable coincidences are inexplicable apart from the fact of Divine inspiration. Written across thousands of centuries, it has but one message: Jesus is the Saviour of all who put their faith in Him.

> Behold! a spotless Victim dies
> My surety on the tree
> The Lamb of God, the Sacrifice
> He gave Himself for me
>
> Whatever curse was mine He bore
> The wormwood and the gall
> There, in that lone mysterious hour
> My cup – He drained it all.

Chapter Twenty-Eight

THE SONGS OF
THE BIBLE

---------------- ❖ ----------------

A radiant, singing Christian is a very powerful Christian
witness. The author can recall a wonderful Christian
lady who always seemed to be singing. She seemed to
radiate a Christian joy as she went about even mundane tasks
with a song in her mouth. Her steady, unruffled joy came as quite
a rebuke to those of us with glum faces, (I should point out that it
was not as though she had life easy.)

In this chapter, we will consider some of the songs of Scripture. The Bible mentions the subject many times, in fact, the book
of Psalms could be considered a hymn book within the Book.
Vast as the songs of Scripture are, we select the following examples:-

1. The Song of the Drunkard

Psalm 69:12 seems to give us a prophetic, 'insider's view'

into the death of Christ. It reads *I am the talk of those who sit in the gate and the drunkards make songs about me.* When Christ was crucified on a public thoroughfare outside the walls of Jerusalem He refused to sip the drugged wine which was given to Him with a view towards numbing the pain (Mark 15:23). Yet our verse lets us imagine the drunken soldiers and jeering crowd around about. Even today, it is well known how alcohol removes people's inhibitions and their mouths give rise to blasphemy against the Lord. A song of blasphemy coming from lips that are designed to praise God is so tragic. It is no wonder that the Bible is adamant that we must be born anew (John 3), that is we must be changed from the inside to the out.

2. The Song of the Disciple

Contrast the song of the drunkard with the Apostle Paul's exhortation: *do not get drunk with wine, for that is debauchery; but be filled with the Spirit, addressing one another in psalms and hymns and spiritual songs, singing and making melody to the Lord with all your heart* (Ephesians 5:18,19).

Is that you? Have you got a song to the Lord in your heart? Have I? If not, why not? Maybe we should ask God for more of His Holy Spirit, as He alone can fill us with the love, joy and peace of God which can only overflow into song. God, according to the book of Job, *gives songs in the night* (Job 35:10). Oh to be able to sing all the time, no matter how dark the circumstances may seem. Paul himself could. Once Paul and his friend Silas were thrown into a dark, dingy, dreadful prison - but the conditions without just could not destroy their condition within, for the record relates that *About midnight Paul and Silas were praying and singing hymns to God, and the prisoners were listening to them* (Acts 16:25). There we see the joy of God in a Christian's heart. It is an inexplicable joy, one which the world can neither give nor take away.

3. The Song of the Delivered

One of the first, if not the first songs of Scripture may be found in Exodus 15. Here, the Israelites had just been delivered by God from slavery in Egypt - a slavery that was both dreadful and painful. What a relief. What a God! What did they do? We read: *Then Moses and all the people of Israel sang this song to the Lord, saying 'I will sing to the Lord, for He has triumphed gloriously, the horse and his rider He has thrown into the sea. The Lord is my strength and my song, and He has become my salvation* . . . (Exodus 15:1,2).

Then there is the Psalmist in Psalm 40. He too knew divine deliverance. He testifies of God: *He drew me up from the desolate pit, out of the miry bog, and set my feet upon a rock, making my steps secure* (Psalm 40:2). But that was not all for *He put a new song in my mouth, a song of praise to our God* (Psalm 40:3).

Singing then is a consequence of salvation – and how much more so if we know the salvation of God in Jesus Christ. No wonder that after the Bible, many Christians' favourite book is their hymnbook. Finally, consider:-

4. The Song of the Delighted

This refers to the song of heaven. What a song to end all songs this will be. If we do not enjoy singing it seems that we will not enjoy heaven! We read that in glory: *they sang a new song* . . . *worthy art Thou* . . . *for Thou wast slain and by Thy blood didst ransom men for God* (Revelation 5:9). What a melody that will be for all those who know the Lord Jesus Christ as their own, personal Saviour. Away with all that brings us down, here on earth, and in with the purest paean of praise from our collective mouths - *a new song.* New, but not absolutely brand new, as if we are believers, we have surely begun to sing that song of praise to the Lamb already – 'This is my story, this is my song, praising my Saviour all the day long.'

So here then are some of the songs of Scripture. There is the song we should not sing. There is the song we can sing. There is the song we ought to sing, and there is the song that we will yet sing if we belong to Jesus now.

> Hark, hark the song the ransomed sing
> a new made song of praise
> The Lord the Lamb they glorify
> and those the strains they raise
>
> 'Glory to Him Who loved us
> and washed us in His blood
> Who cleansed our souls from guilt and sin
> by that pure living flood.'

Chapter Twenty-Nine

THE FRIENDSHIP OF THE BIBLE

❖

True friendship must be one of the greatest gifts, and it is a gift that money cannot buy. *A friend loves at all times, and a brother is born for adversity* reads Proverbs 17:17 – and there is nothing like adversity to make us realise just who are our true friends.

Earthly Friendships with Men

The topic of friendship is rather difficult to discuss. I believe that the number of true friends we have is actually very small, as friends are not to be confused with acquaintances, or those who value us for what we do rather than who we are. Some of us may find the task of forming friendships very difficult, as past experience has taught us not to be too open with everyone, as it can leave us very vulnerable to getting hurt.

The Puritans used to talk about a 'soul friend' or a 'bosom friend', that is, one particular friend who is especially important and close. If you are blessed with one of these, thank God for the friendship, and value it and guard it. Even Jesus Himself, whilst acquainted with many, chose just twelve disciples. From these twelve, three seemed to be closer to Him than others, and of these inner three, John seemed to be the closest to Him. John was literally Jesus' 'bosom friend' (John 13:23).

You may not have thought about it this way before, but the Bible can be considered as a friendship Book. Both human and divine relationships fill its pages. We read in 1 Samuel 18:1 for instance that *the soul of Jonathan was knit to the soul of David, and Jonathan loved him as his own soul.* In the Old Testament we can also read about Daniel and his three companions, and all four stuck together and remained faithful to God in an age and environment of idolatry and apostasy.

Turning to the New Testament, Romans 16 catalogues a huge list of Paul's Christian friends. Of Paul's many friends, his friendship with Timothy is one that stands out. Although they differed in age and experience, they certainly helped and encouraged each other along on their Christian walk and work.

Psalm 41:9 though contains a warning that friends can let us down and disappoint us, as no doubt we can let down and disappoint our friends. The reference seems to be prophetic of Judas' betrayal of Jesus: *Even my bosom friend in whom I trusted, who ate of my bread, has lifted his heel against Me.* Similarly in Psalm 55 David tells how such occurrences of being let down by a supposed friend can be far harder to take than the most venomous barbs of our enemies.

The Bible, then, contains the stories of many human friendships, but its over- riding message is that men and women - sinful men and women like you and me - can come into a relationship with and know the friendship of none less than Almighty God Himself.

Eternal Friendship with God

The friendship of the Lord is for those who fear Him, and He makes known to them His covenant (Psalm 25:14).

The covenant is one of the key words and themes of the Bible. It refers to God's pledge and promise to remain faithful to His people and to be our God through life and death. The main emphasis of the Bible is God's covenant with Abraham, and its outworking to a great multitude of people down through the ages.

In James 2:23 we read that *Abraham believed God and it was reckoned to him as righteousness; and he was called the friend of God.* Whilst Abraham was the founding father of the Hebrew race, he is also in another sense the father of all Christians, as in Galatians 3:29 we read *if you are Christ's, then you are Abraham's offspring, heirs according to promise.* Putting this together then, we may state confidently that we too can know God as our friend if we trust in Him, just as Abraham did. Abraham was far from perfect, just as we are far from perfect. But if we trust in God and believe His promise of salvation in Jesus Christ, we too will be declared righteous by God on behalf of Jesus Christ – and we too can then know the friendship and fellowship with God for which we were made.

In John 15:13 ff. Jesus said *Greater love has no one than this, that a man lay down his life for his friends. You are My friends if you do what I command you.* Whilst Jesus did of course lay down His life for His friends, He actually did more than that: He laid down His life for His enemies. The Bible says *God shows His love for us in that while we were yet sinners Christ died for us . . . while we were enemies we were reconciled to God by the death of His Son* (Romans 5:8,10).

Sin actually makes us God's enemies. We are all sinners by nature, and as such God can only be opposed to us. But the marvel of the Gospel is that God loved sinners so much that He found a way for sinners to be reconciled to Himself. Through

Jesus and His death on the cross for our sins, we can know God's pardon, peace and eternal friendship and fellowship.

Friends are most desirable, but human friendships unfortunately have failure and disappointment built into them. God's friendship however is not like that. He is the God of the covenant. He is faithful and His friendship will not and cannot fail. *There are friends who pretend to be friends, but there is a friend who sticks closer than a brother* (Proverbs 17:24).

> I've found a Friend, O such a Friend!
> He loved me ere I knew Him
> He drew me with the cords of love
> And thus He bound me to Him
> And round my heart still closely twine
> Those ties which nought can sever
> For I am Christ's and He is mine
> For ever and for ever.

Chapter Thirty

THE RESTS OF
THE BIBLE

❖

A night spent in different surroundings and in a different bed can make us appreciate our own bed all the more. Unusual noises can make it difficult to drop off to sleep and our sleep once it does come can be fitful. Then the next morning we may find that we have either a bad back or difficulty in turning our head or both.

Salvation, according to the Bible, can be thought of in terms of a rest. Jesus once gave this wonderful invitation to all who are bowed down by the burden of their sin: *Come to me all who labour and are heavy laden and I will give you rest* (Matthew 11:28). Rest. What a lovely word. In this chapter we will consider four 'rests' of the Bible – rests contained in chapters 3 and 4 of the book of Hebrews.

1. Creation Rest

God rested on the seventh day from all His works (Hebrews 4:4). This takes us back to the book of Genesis, where we read of God's creation of the world in six days and His resting on the seventh, so instituting the Sabbath Day principle. God's creation rest followed on from His perfect, finished work – *And God saw everything that He had made, and behold it was very good* (Genesis 1:31). This creation rest of the Old Testament has an interesting parallel in the 'redemption rest' of the New Testament. Christ rested in the tomb on the Sabbath Day, and this rest followed on from His perfect, finished work of redemption. God finished His work of creation and rested. Jesus similarly said *It is finished* (John 19:30) when He died on the cross, and having accomplished redemption, He rested in the tomb.

2. Canaan Rest

The book of Hebrews also tells us of a rest in the land of Canaan – a rest that never happened. The full story is contained in the Old Testament book of Numbers.

God had promised Israel the land of Canaan – a wonderful land, 'flowing with milk and honey.' Unfortunately though, the Israelites' faith failed. They were unable to possess and enjoy the land God had given them for an inheritance because they were gripped by fear of the giants in the land. *To whom did He swear that they should never enter His rest, but to those who were disobedient? So we see that they were unable to enter because of unbelief* (Hebrews 3:18, 19).

Lack of faith in God can rob us of so much. Lack of faith in this instance saw Israel spending forty years in the barren wilderness instead of the fertile land 'flowing with milk and honey.' Our faith can flicker and waver, but we can be sure that God is faithful and that He is more than sufficient for our insufficiency.

If we are faithless, He remains faithful, for He cannot deny Himself (2 Timothy 2:13).

3. Calvary Rest

Hebrews 4:3 explains that *we who have believed enter that rest* , which means that those who believe in Jesus receive the salvation He has procured at Calvary, and in so believing, enter into the 'rest' of salvation. Calvary rest therefore is the rest of faith. The *Shorter Catechism* explains: 'Faith in Jesus Christ is a saving grace whereby we receive and rest upon Him alone for salvation as He is offered to us in the Gospel.'

Faith in Jesus Christ brings the rest of salvation. Jesus is the complete Saviour Who saves completely. His work of redemption was perfect. Hebrews 10:12 explains *when Christ had offered for all time a single sacrifice for sins He sat down at the right hand of God.* The main difference between the Christian Faith and all other faiths is that other faiths say 'do' whilst the Christian Faith says 'done'. Other Faiths say 'try' whilst the Christian Faith says 'trust'. Other Faiths say 'work' but Jesus says 'rest'.

4. Coming Rest

Paradoxically, Hebrews 4 also says *So then, there remains a Sabbath rest for the people of God; for whoever enters God's rest also ceases from his labours as God did from His* (Hebrews 4:9,10). This refers to the coming glory and eternal rest that awaits the child of God. Then we will be saved from the very presence of sin and not just its penalty and power. *Blessed are those who die in the Lord henceforth. Blessed indeed, says the Spirit, that they may rest from their labours* (Revelation 13:14). This being so, our final quote from Hebrews 4 can only be the exhortation: *Let us therefore strive to enter that rest . . .* (Hebrews 4:11), for

Jesus invites us *Come to Me all who labour and are heavy laden and I will give you rest.*

I heard the voice of Jesus say
'Come unto me and rest'
Lay down thou weary one lay down
Thy head upon my breast
I came to Jesus as I was
Weary and worn and sad
I found in Him a resting place
And He has made me glad.

Chapter Thirty-One

THE LAST CHAPTER
OF THE BIBLE

❖

The famous Agatha Christie 'Whodunit' called *The Mousetrap* has run in London's West End for so long that it is almost a permanent institution. Those who have actually seen it are reluctant to answer the question as to who actually 'does it'. There is kindness in such an action really, as it will keep the fun and suspense should the inquirer ever actually see the play for him or herself. How does the play end? We only know if we actually go and see it for ourselves.

We saw in chapter one of this book that the Bible has 1,189 chapters. The last chapter of the Bible is Revelation 22, and Revelation 22 ends with the words *The grace of the Lord Jesus be with all the saints. Amen* – which is infinitely preferable to the last words of the Old Testament, which are *lest I come and smite the land with a curse* (Malachi 4:6).

I would encourage you to read the last chapter of the Bible as soon as you can. It will, as it were, give you the key to the play, and tie together and resolve the whole plot. Then you will know just where you and the whole universe is heading, and how one day time will change into eternity. Central to all of God's purposes is, of course, His Son the Lord Jesus Christ. So no wonder that in the last chapter of the Bible Jesus proclaims *I am the Alpha and the Omega, the first and the last, the beginning and the end* (Revelation 22:13).

How does the Bible end? You must see for yourself! But for our last thoughts in this book, we will share three points which come out of Revelation 22, the very last chapter of the Bible. These points are a Wonder, a Warning and a Welcome:-

1. A Wonder

The amazing and absolute wonder is that Jesus Christ is coming again – He says so three times in the twenty one verses of the Bible's last chapter. *Surely, I am coming soon* reads the next to last verse. The Second Coming of Christ will be both wonderful and woeful. It will be most wonderful for all those who know Jesus as their friend and Saviour. When He comes again, He will destroy all evil and all that drags us down, and those who love Him now will then rejoice in His presence forevermore. The sobering, woeful aspect of the Second Coming of Christ however is indescribable. The Bible tells of *those who do not obey the Gospel of our Lord Jesus. They shall suffer the punishment of eternal destruction and exclusion from the presence of the Lord* (2 Thessalonians 1:8,9). There could be no worse plight, so how imperative it is that we trust in Jesus now, while we may. The wonder. Jesus is coming again! Revelation 22 also contains though:-

2. A Warning

The last chapter of the Bible includes the difficult verse which reads: *Let the evildoer still be evil, and the filthy still be filthy* . . . (Revelation 22:11) as well as telling us of those described as being *Outside* the heavenly city (Revelation 22:15). These two verses, solemn and stern as they are, show that when we die - or if Jesus returns before we die - our eternal state and destiny will be fixed. If we are excluded from heaven then there will be no second way of entering. There is no passage from hell to heaven after this life – just as, thankfully, there is no passage from heaven to hell. Our attitude to Jesus now, in time, determines where we spend eternity. The Bible exhorts: *Behold, now is the day of salvation* (2 Corinthians 6:2). Who knows where we could be this time next week . . . Life is so frail and fragile. How vital it is to believe in Jesus now and be saved. How foolish to procrastinate with the eternal well-being of our souls. A wonder, a warning, and finally:-

3. A Welcome

On the final page of the Bible there is a welcome. We read the invitation: *Let him who is thirsty come, let him who desires take the water of life without price* (Revelation 22:17). So the invitation to salvation still remains. The last chapter of the Bible pictures salvation as both a cleansing from defilement and also as the most welcome, thirst-quenching water for the thirsty, parched soul. It is Jesus and Jesus alone who cleanses us from sin. It is Jesus and Jesus alone who gives the living water to all who realise their spiritual need and seek Him to satisfy and quench it. The water He gives is costly but free! - *without price.*

So there, in our last chapter, is a taste of the last chapter of the Bible. A wonder, a warning and a welcome. The hymn writer took up the words of welcome and set them into verse, and with these I will close:-

I heard the voice of Jesus say
"Behold I freely give

The living water, thirsty one
stoop down and drink and live'
I came to Jesus and I drank
of that life-giving stream
My thirst was quenched, my soul revived
And now I live in Him.

SOLI DEO GLORIA

EPILOGUE

❖

The Spirit breathes upon the word
And brings the truth to sight
Precepts and promises afford
A sanctifying light

A glory gilds the sacred page
Majestic, like the sun
It gives a light to every age –
It gives, but borrows none

The hand that gave it still supplies
The gracious light and heat
Its truths upon the nations rise
They rise, but never set

Let everlasting thanks be Thine
For such a bright display
As makes a world of darkness shine
With beams of heavenly day

My soul rejoices to pursue
The steps of Him I love
Till glory breaks upon my view
In brighter worlds above.

(William Cowper)

BY THE SAME AUTHOR

WALKING WITH JESUS
By Timothy Cross

Walk where Christ walked, starting with His birth and ending with His ascension into heaven. Walking with Jesus describes and considers ten milestones in the life of Jesus. The ten unforgettable chapters of this book were described by one reviewer as "a devotional classic."

COMFORT FROM THE BIBLE
By Timothy Cross

In this book Dr. Cross illustrates how to draw comfort from the Scriptures in your darkest days. The references he uses are just what you need for any trial you may encounter. God's Word is the only source we need to lift the veil of depression, the weight of sorrow, or the load of responsibility.

SCENT FROM HEAVEN
By Timothy Cross

Can any fragrance be as sweet as the loveliness of Christ? In this rich, devotional, typological study, the author points out that our blessing derives from Christ's bruising. As fragrant plants do not yield their sweet perfume unless they are crushed, likewise, if our Saviour had not been crushed at Calvary, He could not have given His sweetest pardon.

MY FATHER'S HOUSE
By Timothy Cross

The glory that awaits the child of God is unspeakable and unimaginable. Beautifully pictured in this book is a small glimpse of what heaven holds for us. After a peek into heaven, you will view your day-to-day tasks in a different light.